Government Failure
versus Market Failure

Government Failure versus Market Failure

Microeconomics Policy Research and Government Performance

Clifford Winston

AEI-BROOKINGS JOINT CENTER
FOR REGULATORY STUDIES
Washington, D.C.

Government Failure versus Market Failure may be ordered from:
Brookings Institution Press, 1775 Massachusetts Avenue, N.W.
Washington, D.C. 20036. 1-800/537-5487 or 410/516-6956;
E-mail: hfscustserv@press.jhu.edu; www.brookings.edu

Library of Congress Cataloging-in-Publication data
Winston, Clifford, 1952–
Government failure versus market failure : microeconomics policy
research and government performance / Clifford Winston.
   p.   cm.
Includes bibliographical references and index.
ISBN-13: 978-0-8157-9390-8 (hardcover : alk. paper)
ISBN-10: 0-8157-9390-1 (hardcover : alk. paper)
ISBN-13: 978-0-8157-9389-2 (pbk. : alk. paper)
ISBN-10: 0-8157-9389-8 (pbk. : alk. paper)
1. Industrial policy.   2. Microeconomics.   I. Title.
HD3611.W555 2006
338.5—dc22   2006024066

2 4 6 8 9 7 5 3 1

The paper used in this publication meets minimum requirements of the
American National Standard for Information Sciences—Permanence of Paper
for Printed Library Materials: ANSI Z39.48-1992.

Typeset in Adobe Garamond

Composition by R. Lynn Rivenbark
Macon, Georgia

Printed by R. R. Donnelley
Harrisonburg, Virginia

To Joan, HJ, and TH

forever in Manoku

Contents

Foreword

How can economists help improve public policy? One way is by taking a serious look at the effectiveness of different kinds of policy interventions. That is exactly what Clifford Winston does in this important book assessing market failure and government failure. Winston's careful and comprehensive analysis of the empirical evidence on the economic impact of government policies to correct market failures leads to some troubling insights. He finds that government interventions frequently occur when no significant market failure exists. In addition, many policies aimed at addressing market failures that do exist could have corrected them at significantly lower cost. Winston covers a number of policy areas in this book, including regulation and antitrust, information and externalities, and public production.

It is encouraging that Winston finds some evidence that policymakers are pursuing fewer inefficient policies in certain areas and that they have implemented some beneficial reforms. For example, policymakers are less likely to implement price controls in response to excess demand for commodities such as gasoline. In addition, they are more inclined to appreciate the benefits of deregulation of specific industries such as airlines. They are also more likely to apply market-based approaches to achieving environmental objectives—a case in point being the successful program to reduce acid rain. A key recommendation Winston offers is to experiment

with more market-oriented policies for addressing externalities and for providing public services and infrastructure.

This volume is one in a series commissioned by the AEI-Brookings Joint
Center for Regulatory Studies to contribute to the continuing debate over
the appropriate role of government and government regulation. The series
addresses several fundamental issues, including the impact of government
policies, the design of effective reforms, and the political and institutional
forces that affect reform.

Like all Joint Center publications, this monograph can be freely down-
loaded at www.aei-brookings.org. We encourage educators to distribute
these materials to their students by asking them to download publications
directly from our website. The views expressed here are those of the authors
and should not be attributed to the trustees, officers, or staff members of
the American Enterprise Institute or the Brookings Institution.

ROBERT W. HAHN
ROBERT E. LITAN
AEI-Brookings Joint Center for Regulatory Studies

Acknowledgments

I have benefited from comments and suggestions from many people. In particular, I would like to thank Jack Calfee, Menzie Chinn, Robert Crandall, Darius Gaskins, Richard Geddes, Robert Hahn, James Hamilton, Andrew Kleit, Robert Litan, Steven Morrison, Sam Peltzman, Dennis Sheehan, Kenneth Small, Timothy Taylor, and Scott Wallsten. Linda Cohen, Lee Friedman, and W. Kip Viscusi provided exceptionally constructive reviews of the manuscript. Ashley Langer, Vikram Maheshri, Alise Upitis, and David Zipper provided much more than research assistance. Jesse Gurman provided much more than research verification. Finally, I am grateful to Martha Gottron for her careful editing.

1 | *Introduction*

The Aim of Science is not to open the door to infinite wisdom, but to set a limit to infinite error.

BERTOLT BRECHT

Shortly after he took office, President George W. Bush nominated Harvard professor John D. Graham to head the Office of Information and Regulatory Affairs within the Office of Management and Budget. Graham was known to be a strong advocate of using cost-benefit analysis to assess and reform environmental, health, and safety regulation. If, for example, the Environmental Protection Agency (EPA) proposed a regulation that saved 100 lives but at a cost of $1 billion per life, Graham would oppose the regulation and encourage the EPA to craft an alternative that could save these lives at a much lower cost that was aligned with conventional estimates of the "value of life." Or if the National Highway and Traffic Safety Administration (NHTSA) proposed a regulation that forced automakers to adopt a specific technology to reduce fuel consumption but the resulting benefits were less than the increased costs to automakers of implementing the technology, Graham would oppose the regulation on the grounds that its social net benefits were negative.

To an economist, these positions are eminently reasonable. But some commentators and policymakers are outright dismissive of policy assessments based on cost-benefit analysis, apparently willing to substitute good intentions—or their own political agenda—for analysis. Indeed, Senator Dick Durbin's response to Graham's nomination was an op-ed in the *Washington Post* on July 16, 2001, entitled "Graham Flunks the Cost-Benefit Test," while Georgetown University law professor Liza Heinzerling expressed her views in the *Los Angeles Times* on July 19, 2001, with an op-ed entitled "Don't Put the Fox in Charge of the Hens."

Such refusals to acknowledge that government interventions can have costs as well as benefits raise a fundamental concern about whether U.S. government policy is truly enhancing microeconomic efficiency—that is, the degree to which our economic system meets the material wants, as measured by quantity and quality, of its members. Microeconomic efficiency, or Pareto optimality, is achieved when it is impossible to make one person better off without making someone else worse off. In theory, government policy seeks to improve microeconomic efficiency by correcting a market failure, defined by Bator (1958) as the failure of a system of price-market institutions to stop "undesirable" activities, where the desirability of an activity is evaluated relative to some explicit economic welfare maximization problem. Accordingly, a market failure can be defined as an equilibrium allocation of resources that is not Pareto optimal—the potential causes of which may be market power, natural monopoly, imperfect information, externalities, or public goods.

On what basis is one to conclude that a policy to correct a market failure is as successful as possible? The first consideration is whether government has any reason to intervene in a market: Is there evidence of a serious market failure to correct? The second is whether government policy is at least improving market performance: Is it reducing the economic inefficiency, or "deadweight" loss, from market failure? Of course, the policy could be an "expensive" success by generating benefits that exceed costs, but incurring excessive costs to obtain the benefits. Hence, the final consideration is whether government policy is optimal: Is it efficiently correcting the market failure and maximizing economic welfare?

Government failure, then, arises when government has created inefficiencies because it should not have intervened in the first place or when it could have solved a given problem or set of problems more efficiently, that is, by generating greater net benefits. In other words, the theoretical benchmark of Pareto optimality could be used to assess government performance just as it is used to assess market performance. Of course, the ideal of a completely efficient market is rarely, if ever, observed in practice. From a policy perspective, market failure should be a matter of concern when market performance significantly deviates from the appropriate efficiency benchmark. Similarly, a government failure should call a government intervention into question when economic welfare is actually reduced or when resources are allocated in a manner that significantly deviates from an appropriate efficiency benchmark.

Economic theory can suggest optimal public policies to correct market failures, but the effect of government's market failure policies on economic welfare can be assessed only with *empirical evidence*. For more than a century, the primary market failure policies implemented by government have included antitrust policy and economic regulation to curb market power, so-called social regulatory policies to address imperfect information and externalities, and public financing of socially desirable services that the private sector would not provide. Initially, economists assessed these policies on conceptual grounds, culminating in Friedman's (1962) classic attack questioning government's role in almost all areas of economic life. Schultze (1977) was one of the first to systematically raise doubts about the effectiveness of government policies based on the limited empirical evidence that was available. Wolf (1979) introduced the term nonmarket failure to indicate some type of government failure and suggested that government failure may be of the same order of importance as market failure.

An additional thirty years of empirical evidence on the efficacy of market failure policies initiated primarily by the federal government, but also by the states, suggests that the welfare cost of government failure may be considerably greater than that of market failure. More specifically, the evidence suggests that policymakers have attempted to correct market failures with policies designed to affect either consumer or firm behavior, or both, or to allocate resources. Some policies have forced the U.S. economy to incur costs in situations where no serious market failure exists, while others, in situations where costly market failures do exist, could have improved resource allocation in a much more efficient manner.

Government failures appear to be explained by the self-correcting nature of some market failures, which makes government intervention unnecessary; by the short-sightedness, inflexibility, and conflicting policies of government agencies; and by political forces that allow well-defined interest groups to influence elected and unelected officials to initiate and maintain inefficient policies that enable the interest groups to accrue economic rents.

My negative assessment is not intended to suggest that all microeconomic policies are ineffective or to spur defenders of an active government to search for evidence of policies that work. My objective is to focus attention on how current policy, in broad terms, can be improved. This is not a futile exercise because in the past few decades government has become somewhat less inclined to pursue inefficient policies and has initiated some beneficial reforms. For example, U.S. policymakers are less likely today than they once were to try to correct a perceived market imperfection by instituting (counterproductive) price regulations such as milk price supports or oil price controls. Similarly, in some cases policymakers have enhanced economic welfare by withdrawing their market failure policy in favor of a market solution (for example, economic deregulation) and by designing a framework that makes effective use of market forces to reduce the inefficiencies caused by a market failure (for example, well-designed emissions trading programs). Further applications of and experiments with market-oriented policies to address externalities and public financing of socially desirable activities are likely to reveal that such policies are far superior to current policies at remedying market failures in an efficient manner.

Although researchers have identified serious flaws in other market failure policies, such as antitrust, patents, and certain information policies, the profession's empirical knowledge is too limited to permit confident suggestions about how policy in these areas can be significantly improved. Thus, additional research is clearly needed to help guide the formulation of appropriate policy in these areas.

Although my assessment and policy recommendations are based on a broad and thorough synthesis of the available empirical evidence on the economic effects of market failure policies, it is vital for the economics policy community—including researchers and policymakers—to continue the task of accumulating, building, and drawing on this evidence so that future policy debates do not have to begin from "square one." Over the past few decades, the profession has begun to understand which policies have been successful and which have not, as well as why policymakers fail to pursue socially desirable reforms. The gap between the plethora of policies recommended by economists to correct market failure and mitigate government failure and the policies the government has pursued should only encourage—not discourage—the profession's efforts to assemble and disseminate a useful empirical base of knowledge about the performance of government's microeconomic policies. In isolated instances, public officials have shown the capacity to learn from economic research and improve their policies. A more comprehensive body of evidence should lead to much-better-informed action and, more broadly, to socially desirable outcomes.

The disappointing outcome of government's current microeconomic policies should be of great concern to everyone interested in public affairs regardless of political persuasion or occupation. By documenting government's performance and indicating how it can be improved, I hope to do more than set a "limit to infinite error."

2 | *Methodological Perspective*

conomists began systematically using the tools of applied welfare economics, also known as cost-benefit analysis, as early as the 1960s to empirically assess government policies designed to correct market failures. Harberger (1971) gave applied welfare economics a theoretical framework that was distilled into three postulates: benefits and costs to consumers should be calculated using consumer surplus; benefits and costs to producers should be calculated using producer surplus; benefits and costs accruing to each group should normally be added without regard to the individual(s) to whom they accrue.

Although Harberger's framework has been refined, many empirical assessments of public policies calculate costs and benefits using (some measure of) consumer and producer surplus.[1] Policies that, in theory, are intended to improve economic efficiency are evaluated by determining

---

1. As is well known, consumer surplus is an inexact measure of welfare change because it assumes that the marginal utility of income is constant. Compensating and equivalent variations are exact welfare measures that do not make this assumption, but there are no theoretical grounds for choosing between them because they do not resolve the index number problem—a policy that affects prices can be assessed by comparing consumer utility at the new prices with what utility would have been under the initial prices or by comparing consumer utility at the initial prices with what utility would have been under the new prices. Willig (1976) derived bounds to calculate the approximation error using consumer surplus, and Hausman (1981) developed a procedure to estimate compensating variations. Hausman's method has been used in some policy assessments, but the vast majority use consumer surplus.

their net benefits and identifying the winners and losers. Kaplow and Shavell (2001) have shown that any policy evaluation that incorporates factors beyond efficiency and redistribution necessarily violates the Pareto principle by allowing for the possibility that the new system of evaluation supports policy changes in which all members of society are made worse off. For some policies, researchers have sought to identify the benefits of a particular government intervention, say, the Occupational Safety and Health Administration's safety standards for workplaces, noting that implementing the policy generates enforcement and compliance costs that need to be included in a full assessment.

Practitioners of applied welfare economics have, in general, treated all individuals equally, while recognizing that when some people organize to form a particular interest group their political influence can shed light on why inefficient policies are implemented and whether alternative policies are feasible. Researchers have rarely attempted to justify market failure policies solely on redistributive grounds, but they have indicated when policymakers are likely to oppose efficient market failure policies because they may harm individuals with low incomes.

The heart of Harberger's framework is that firms and consumers are self-interested agents who respond rationally to public policies.[2] As pointed out by Varian (1993), people may behave irrationally in laboratory studies by violating transitivity, expected utility maximization, and elementary probability, but this behavior is sufficiently rare in actual markets that many economists are willing to advocate only policies that assume people behave rationally. The growing research in behavioral economics may challenge this position by empirically confirming that agents often depart from rational behavior in particular settings, but policies based on such behavior will need to be implemented and assessed before we can conclude that they have merit.

Since Harberger's article, microeconomic policy evaluations have been strengthened by advances in econometric modeling, greater computational capabilities, experimental economics, and the growing availability of data sets covering a wide range of consumers' and firms' economic behavior. Any policy evaluation amounts to a *counterfactual* analysis where the economic effects of a public policy are isolated by using a multivariate analy-

2. There is a growing literature that assesses whether government agencies' policies are consistent with the recommendations of cost-benefit analysis and, given that they are not, whether agencies should be required to meet this standard; see, for example, Posner (2001) and Sunstein (2001).

sis to hold constant all other variables that are unrelated to the public policy but that could affect policy outcomes.

I summarize in detail the effect of policies whose primary objective in principle is to correct a market failure. As noted, the policies that I assess are antitrust and regulatory policies, information and externality policies, and public production. The nature of this exercise invariably involves judgments about the evidence that I report, the specific policies that I assess, and how I resolve methodological disputes. I therefore clarify my approach to these matters.

Evidence

My primary source of evidence consists of scholarly assessments of federal policies that are published in journals and books. (To facilitate comparisons of the welfare effects of different policies, I report all empirical estimates in 2000 dollars, unless otherwise indicated.) I draw on the research of all scholars to report the most recent findings on the economic effects of a market failure policy, but not at the expense of suppressing current or historical disagreement. My search of the evidence is not limited to policy failures; I report success stories, but few of them emerged from my search.

I also draw on a handful of studies, performed by the government, containing peer-reviewed evidence that was not published in a scholarly outlet. For the most part, however, I do not use studies conducted by the government. As pointed out by Hahn (1996), these studies can be biased, inconsistent, and technically flawed because they have not been subject to review by appropriate scholars. Hahn even suggests that some government agencies do not appear to trust the numbers produced by government assessments of their own policies. Finally, I supplement some of the scholarly empirical evidence with useful descriptive information reported by the media.

Policies

I focus on federal rather than state policies because federal policies have received more attention in the literature and they are concerned with national welfare. Some state policies may seek to promote the interest of a particular state at the expense of national welfare. Of course, in some instances the states may be able to develop and implement policies that are more effective than those that have been enacted by the federal government. The strengths and weaknesses of federal versus state policies raise the issue of federalism and whether market failure policies, as well as other policies, should be implemented at the federal or lower levels. I do not have sufficient evidence to address this issue here. In a few cases, however, I report the effects of both federal and state policies on consumer welfare.

As noted, the scope of this study is limited to policies that are intended to enhance microeconomic efficiency. Microeconomic efficiency ignores the distribution of income; thus, I distinguish market failure policies from government interventions whose explicit objective is to redistribute income from one group of citizens to another group of citizens to pursue a social goal. The primary social goals in the United States include reducing poverty, ensuring fairness in labor markets, and providing merit goods—that is, goods and services that American society believes every citizen is entitled to regardless of whether he or she can afford them. In contrast to efficient market failure policies, social goals policies are *not* intended to meet the standard of Pareto optimality by making someone better off without making anyone worse off. Of course, in certain situations it is not completely clear whether a policy is intended to enhance microeconomic efficiency or achieve a social goal. For example, education subsidies seek to provide a merit good, although the subsidies may generate a positive externality by raising the skills of the nation's workforce or correcting possible failures in capital markets. However, the scholarly assessments of education subsidies have primarily evaluated them on the grounds of whether they are achieving a social goal in an efficient manner rather than whether they are efficiently correcting a potential market failure.

In any case, I argue later that assessments of market failure and social goals policies have often identified similar flaws in government performance. In addition, I briefly discuss how, in practice, these policies often conflict and weaken each other.

Disputes

Notwithstanding the potential for methodological disputes to arise when microeconomic policies are evaluated, my assessment of the empirical evidence reveals a surprising degree of consensus about the paucity of major policy successes in correcting a market failure efficiently.[3] In contrast to the sharp divisions that characterize debates over the efficacy of macroeconomic policy interventions, I found only a handful of empirical studies that disagree about whether a particular government policy had enhanced efficiency by substantially correcting a market failure. I identify those studies and offer my perspective on the debate.

Generally, my fundamental conclusions are not influenced by studies that use a particular methodology. In fact, researchers who used vastly different methodological techniques to assess specific policies often reached very similar conclusions. Thus, I do not assess methodological approaches or attempt to identify pitfalls that future market failure policy assessments should avoid.

Finally, although I recognize that policy assessments must account for institutional complexities and governmental entities that shape policy implementation and affect performance, I limit my discussion to the theoretical motivation for each policy, its essential features, and its economic effects. Viscusi, Harrington, and Vernon (2005) offer a wealth of institutional detail on the history and current state of antitrust, economic regulation, and social regulation and the federal agencies that implement these policies. Institutional background on public production is available in several sources that I cite later. My primary focus in the next three chapters is on the bottom line: To what extent does a market failure policy improve social welfare? In the chapters that follow, I synthesize the evidence, indicate how policymaking has improved, offer policy recommendations, and suggest how the microeconomics research agenda and scholars' engagement with the policy community can be improved.

3. Academics tend to be social critics, so there may be a fundamental bias in published economics research that favors negative conclusions about government performance. However, academics, especially economists, are contentious individuals who are unlikely to shy away from the opportunity to challenge other researchers' findings simply because they will be identified as supporting government policy.

3 | *Market Power: Antitrust Policy and Economic Regulation*

In the textbook model of perfect competition, firms earn a normal market rate of return in the long run. Of course, some firms may have superior technologies and management, which enable them to earn an above-normal rate of return for an indeterminate length of time. But when a firm attempts to capture consumer surplus by engaging in illegal conduct to monopolize a market or by abusing its market power, government policy, as codified in the antitrust laws, can improve consumer welfare by stopping these actions and discouraging other firms from engaging in such behavior.

A market's technological characteristics may give rise to natural monopoly, an unusual situation where social costs are minimized when one (well-behaved) firm serves the market. Competition under these conditions could therefore result in industrywide bankruptcy or a monopoly survivor. Because an unregulated monopolist is likely to extract consumer surplus at the expense of total welfare, government policy in the form of economic regulation can improve economic welfare by setting more efficient prices for the monopoly provider and preventing other firms from entering the market, albeit with adverse incentives for innovation. Optimal prices could be set either at marginal cost with a subsidy or tax that enables the regulated monopolist to earn a normal return or at Ramsey prices that satisfy a break-even constraint. (Under Ramsey pricing, the percentage markup of prices above marginal cost is inversely related to consumers' demand elasticities to minimize the welfare loss from inefficient substitution.)

Although antitrust and economic regulation are motivated by different concerns, they share a common theme in that both seek to move a market closer to the competitive ideal. I therefore assess both in the same chapter.

The theoretical justification for antitrust laws and economic regulation does not imply that government intervention is necessary to curb market power and improve economic efficiency—or that it has done so in practice. Nor is intervention warranted simply because one can cite examples of firms that have colluded or can identify markets that are subject to scale economies over a wide range of output. Policies to curb market power can be justified only by evidence that they can and do increase output and thereby raise social welfare. However, the summary findings that I draw from the current state of the available scholarly evidence are:

> Antitrust policies toward monopolization, mergers, and collusion have done little to raise consumer welfare, while economic regulation of agricultural products and international trade has produced large deadweight losses in the process of transferring resources from consumers to producers.

Antitrust Policy

U.S. antitrust policy is the responsibility of the Department of Justice (DOJ) and the Federal Trade Commission (FTC). The Justice Department enforces Section 1 of the Sherman Antitrust Act of 1890 prohibiting contracts, combinations, and conspiracies in restraint of trade; Section 2 of the Sherman Act prohibiting actions to monopolize or attempts to monopolize markets through anticompetitive means; and, along with the FTC, Section 7 of the Clayton Act of 1914 (amended in 1950) prohibiting mergers between firms that threaten to lessen competition substantially in any line of commerce.[1]

1. The Clayton Act also prohibits firms from engaging in tying arrangements and competing firms from having overlapping boards of directors. The FTC may also initiate cases under Section 5 of the Federal Trade Commission Act for "unfair methods of competition," thereby providing it with the ability to combat abuses that DOJ attacks under Sections 1 and 2 of the Sherman Act. Finally, the Robinson-Patman Act's prohibition against price discrimination has rarely been enforced during the

It is difficult to provide a summary measure of how competitive U.S. industries are at any point in time, but the available evidence does not suggest that the nation's economy is suffering from any serious underlying anticompetitive problems. For example, Pashigian (2000) followed common practice in defining an imperfectly competitive market as having a four-firm concentration ratio above 70 percent and found that in 1992 only 46 out of 398 Standard Industry Classification four-digit U.S. manufacturing industries met that criterion.[2] (Preliminary evidence based on 2002 U.S. Census data shows a decline in the extent of imperfectly competitive markets in manufacturing industries.) In addition, the theme that domestic markets are highly competitive is consistent with the common finding that the U.S. economy has experienced only a small deadweight loss from noncompetitive pricing. Harberger's (1954) initial estimate of a deadweight loss due to monopoly of roughly 0.1 percent of GDP (gross domestic product) has been revisited by several authors. Cowling and Mueller (1978) found a much larger deadweight loss than other researchers because they included advertising expenses as part of the welfare losses. More recent estimates summarized by Ferguson (1988) indicate a figure of about 1 percent of GDP. This estimate includes transfers from consumers to firms, but it also includes price distortions from regulations and trade protection (see below). The relevant issue here is therefore whether the apparent absence of serious anticompetitive problems in the United States is the result of or largely independent of more than a century of antitrust policy directed at monopolization, collusion, and mergers.[3]

---

past twenty years, while the application of the Sherman Act against resale price maintenance was substantially reduced in 1997.

2. The Standard Industry Classification is a U.S. government system for classifying industries by a four-digit code (3575, for example, refers to computer terminals). Manufacturing accounts for about 16 percent of GDP. Comprehensive concentration data are not readily available for other sectors of the private economy. Furthermore, similar to many manufacturing industries, many service industries are global in scope.

3. Firms can also be indicted under the antitrust laws for anticompetitive behavior that enables them to become the sole buyer of a product. In practice, such monopsony power has primarily been a concern of public policy because a sole employer in a market tends to pay employees below the value of their marginal product. But instead of prosecuting firms that set monopsony wages, the government, as codified in the National Labor Relations Act, has guaranteed the right of employees to organize and engage in collective (union) bargaining with their employers to determine wages and other terms of employment. Collective bargaining has raised wages, but it cannot be justified as a counter to monopsony power in the labor market because such power is rare and not much of a factor in low wage rates (Boal and Ransom 1997). Unions have also been successful in garnering fringe benefits for workers

Monopolization

Consumers would be expected to benefit when the government prevailed in a monopolization case and the court was entrusted with providing competitive relief (such as divestiture). Crandall and Winston (2003) synthesized evidence on landmark cases where this occurred, including Standard Oil (1911), American Tobacco (1911), Alcoa (1945), Paramount (1948), and United Shoe Machinery (1954), and consistently found that the court's relief failed to increase competition and reduce consumer prices. Crandall and Winston also found that more recent antitrust enforcement of monopolization, including cases against IBM, Safeway, A&P, and Blue-Chip Stamps, has failed to generate consumer gains.

A possible exception to their findings is the 1984 breakup of AT&T, which followed a 1974 monopolization case. But the key aspect of the decree that gave rise to the growth in long-distance telephone competition and lower rates—namely, Bell companies were required to modify their switching facilities to provide equal access to all long-distance carriers—could have been promulgated by the Federal Communications Commission (FCC) without the intervention of the antitrust authorities. The FCC, however, was trying to block MCI from competing in ordinary long-distance services when the Justice Department filed suit against AT&T in 1974. Thus, antitrust policy was not necessary to restrain a monopolist from engaging in restrictive practices to block competition; rather it was necessary to overcome anticompetitive policies by another federal regulatory agency.[4]

In the absence of regulatory failure, the large costs of breaking up AT&T could have been avoided. These costs include restructuring AT&T to consummate the breakup, legal enforcement costs, and denying the efficiencies of vertical integration (Crandall 2005b). Indeed, the telecommunications industry has evolved into a competitive struggle among at least

---

such as health insurance, pensions, and paid vacations, and in reducing transaction costs in the determination of wages. But unions have also reduced productivity growth and firm profitability; thus economists have not reached a consensus on their net benefits to society (Booth 1995).

4. AT&T was unable to obtain broad antitrust immunity because the courts have held that such immunity would be appropriate only where there was actual or potential conflict between FCC regulation and the antitrust laws or where regulatory controls on entry and price precluded AT&T's exercise of monopoly power (Kellogg, Thorne, and Huber 1992).

three vertically integrated technologies: fixed wire telephone companies (excluding AT&T!), cable television companies, and wireless carriers.

Given the protracted length of a monopolization case (some of the cases noted earlier took more than a decade to resolve), federal antitrust actions are likely to lag far behind market developments and thus be less effective than markets in stimulating competition. Alternatively, notwithstanding a court's intentions, the relief obtained by the government and embedded in a court's decree may simply have a negligible practical impact on consumers.[5]

Collusion

Although the existing evidence is far from comprehensive or definitive, economists have yet to find that antitrust prosecution of collusion has led to significantly lower consumer prices. Sproul (1993) analyzed a sample of twenty-five price-fixing cases between 1973 and 1984. He argued that if the cartel had raised prices above competitive levels, then prosecution should have lowered them. Controlling for other influences, however, he found that prices *rose* an average of 7 percent four years after an indictment. Sproul also found that prices rose, on average, even if one used a starting point during the investigation but before the indictment.

Retrospective assessments of specific price-fixing prosecutions have also found that consumers did not benefit from the actions that were taken, including a price-fixing indictment against bakers (Newmark 1988) and a consent decree that prohibited airlines from announcing the ending dates of their fare promotions, which ostensibly could facilitate collusion (Morrison and Winston 1996). In 2001 Sotheby's and Christie's settled a price-fixing suit, which alleged among other things that in 1995 the two auction houses began conspiring to elevate their sales commissions. Apparently, the

---

5. The merits of the *Microsoft* case are not yet clear, but its drawbacks are consistent with the problems of other monopolization cases. First, it has turned out to be a lengthy case. The U.S. antitrust suit was filed in May 1998 and some private actions are still unsettled. Microsoft also faces a major antitrust challenge in Europe. By the time the case is fully resolved, the information technology market is likely to have changed substantially and Microsoft's dominant position may be eroded. Second, challenges to a modest remedy were rejected in 2004. But the remedy has left both sides questioning the point of the case. Evans, Nichols, and Schmalensee (2005) contend that the remedy is likely to contribute future benefits to consumers but acknowledge that their position is not based on a careful calculation of costs and benefits that accounts for compliance and litigation costs.

settlement had little effect because Sotheby's 2003 revenues (mainly from commissions) as a percent of its auction revenues (18.2 percent based on Securities and Exchange Commission filings) actually exceeded its 1993 revenues as a percent of auction revenues (17.7 percent). To be sure, it is possible to identify other successful price-fixing prosecutions, such as the 1990s prosecution of the international vitamins cartel, but no serious academic study has shown that these cases have led to significantly lower prices for a protracted period.

Justice Department enforcement may be ineffective because it is primarily prosecuting firms that are engaged in joint activities that involve other goals besides raising prices. For example, Sproul suggests that a cartel may reduce costs through shared advertising and research, which may tend to reduce prices rather than to increase them. Another possibility is that a cartel may be pursuing distributional goals. For instance, MIT and Ivy League colleges established a tradition of coordinating their needs-based financial aid decisions. The schools claimed that the so-called Overlap process enabled them to concentrate their scarce financial aid resources on needy students without affecting their total tuition revenues. The government claimed that the schools were conspiring on financial aid policies to reduce aid and raise revenues. Carlton, Bamberger, and Epstein (1995) found that the Overlap process did not have a statistically significant effect on the amount of student aid but that it did result in a larger share of revenues being awarded to low-income students.

Mergers

Mergers may harm or benefit consumers. Mergers that enable firms to acquire market power result in higher prices, while mergers that enable firms to realize operational and managerial efficiencies reduce costs and thereby lower prices.[6] In certain markets, a merged entity may stimulate competition and reduce markups over costs. The effectiveness of merger policy therefore depends on how well the antitrust authorities can distinguish procompetitive mergers from anticompetitive ones.

---

6. Viscusi, Harrington, and Vernon (2005, chapter 7) present graphical depictions of the potential costs and benefits of a merger.

Apparently, the authorities cannot evaluate mergers in a way that systematically enhances consumer welfare. Evidence from the finance literature indicates that mergers that were challenged by the DOJ and the FTC were in general not anticompetitive and would have been efficient had they been allowed to go through (Eckbo 1992). Mergers that were challenged or opposed by antitrust regulators but were consummated anyway have often resulted in gains for consumers (Schuman, Reitzes, and Rogers 1997; Morrison 1996). Finally, Crandall and Winston (2003) analyzed the effects of merger policy on price-cost margins and found that the antitrust authorities have primarily attacked mergers that would enhance efficiency, either by blocking them in court or allowing them to proceed only if the merger partners agreed to conditions that turned out to raise their costs.

Deterrence

The strongest argument in support of antitrust policy is that it may enhance consumer welfare by *deterring* firms from engaging in illegal practices that would ultimately raise prices. Unfortunately, the beneficial effects of deterrence are difficult to observe—for example, the price-fixing arrangement that never takes place, the merger to monopoly that is not consummated, and the predatory strategy that is not attempted.

International comparisons have therefore been used to shed some light on the effect of antitrust on deterring monopolization and anticompetitive mergers. Stigler (1966) compared concentration in specific industries in the United States with the same industries in England, which at the time of his study did not have a public policy against concentration of control, and concluded that the Sherman Act has had a very modest effect in reducing U.S. concentration. Eckbo (1992) explored whether the antitrust laws deterred potentially anticompetitive mergers by estimating whether the probability that a horizontal merger was anticompetitive was higher in Canada, where until 1985 mergers were allowed to take place in a legal environment that was effectively unconstrained, than in the United States. Based on this comparison he rejected the hypothesis that the U.S. antitrust laws were deterring anticompetitive mergers.

Firms and individuals convicted of price-fixing are subject to federal criminal penalties and also vulnerable to private suits for treble damages.

Block, Nold, and Sidak (1981) offered evidence that such class actions were the strongest deterrence against collusion. Recently, the Antitrust Division of the Department of Justice has attempted to strengthen deterrence by imposing higher fines on corporations for price fixing and by expanding the use of corporate leniency for firms that disclose their role in a conspiracy and cooperate with the government. These policies may be thought to benefit consumers, but Kobayashi (2002) cautioned that they may lead to overdeterrence, which would induce excessive investments in monitoring and prevention, raise production costs, and result in higher consumer prices. Apparently, some firms have not been deterred from colluding because the Justice Department continues to bring price-fixing cases. While it is possible that DOJ has succeeded in deterring the most serious instances of price fixing and has therefore been increasingly prosecuting marginal cases, this surmise has not been documented.

In sum, theory and evidence indicate that the highly competitive U.S. environment has caused monopolies to be eroded, made it difficult for firms to maintain harmful collusive agreements, and led to mergers that either provide efficiency benefits or fail to enhance firm value. In contrast, antitrust policy's deterrence effects are in theory mixed and in practice not clear. Firms could be discouraged from engaging in socially beneficial activities, such as cost sharing, for fear of misguided prosecution, or they could be deterred from anticompetitive behavior. It is critical to measure the extent of each action. As I argue later, the inability to do so precludes strong policy recommendations for improving antitrust policy.

A Credibility Check

Many readers are likely to question whether the current state of the available evidence leads to a uniformly critical appraisal of market failure policies in general and of antitrust policy in particular. I maintain that it does, but I also acknowledge that my negative assessment of antitrust policy is not shared by all who have written on the topic. It is therefore useful to consider how those who believe that antitrust policy has had positive effects support their position empirically. In response to Crandall and Winston, Baker (2003) offered a cost-benefit analysis of antitrust enforcement as support for the social desirability of the activity. He argued that the annual costs of enforcement were small, roughly $1 billion, and that the potential benefits were likely to be much greater—as much as $100 billion a year. But Baker did not obtain his estimate of benefits from empirical assessments of the effects of actual antitrust cases on consumers. Instead, he claimed that they could be large because price-fixing conspiracies were quite costly to consumers (for example, collusion among vitamin producers cost consumers at least $100 million). However, in the absence of hard evidence that antitrust actions have actually reduced the costs of collusion to consumers or benefited them in other ways, it is inappropriate to claim that the consumer gains from such actions exceed enforcement costs—especially because these costs are likely to approach several billion dollars annually when one accounts for lawyers' fees, payments to consultants, opportunity costs of managers and employees who participate in a firm's defense, and so on.

Kouliavtsev (2004) supported antitrust policy on similar grounds as Baker and cited some evidence that antitrust policy had deterred mergers between 1959 and 1972 that would have been harmful to consumers. But this evidence was based on the assumption that *any* increase in concentration in a product market increases the price-cost margin. Despite this rather heroic assumption, the fifty-nine horizontal merger cases that provided the basis for Kouliavtsev's favorable assessment generated gains in allocative efficiency that were smaller than the enforcement costs created by the action. Thus, it is difficult for Kouliavtsev to maintain a favorable assessment of antitrust on cost-benefit grounds.

Finally, Werden (2004) tried to cast merger policy in a better light than documented here, but he failed to provide favorable academic assessments of actual antitrust cases. To be sure, there are important gaps in our knowledge of the economic effects of antitrust policy that merit the profession's attention. Nonetheless, the verdict of the available empirical evidence is that current policy provides negligible benefits to consumers that fall far short of enforcement costs.[7]

---

7. Stigler (1982) raised concerns that the economic profession's growing support for antitrust was not based on systematic evidence of its economic effects. In a memorandum dated March 23, 2005, then U.S. Department of Justice Antitrust Division assistant attorney general R. Hewitt Pate proposed that the Antitrust Modernization Commission consider "engaging respected experts . . . to design a rigorous study of the effects of antitrust enforcement." Pate noted that the Crandall and Winston article was one of the inspirations for this proposal, notwithstanding the challenges to that paper summarized here (www.amc.gov/pdf/meetings/empirical.pdf).

Economic Regulation

Beginning with the 1887 Interstate Commerce Act that regulated the rail-roads, the federal government has used its legal power to control pricing, entry, and exit in industries where competition allegedly was not workable because large scale economies would cause firms to undercut each other's prices until they were either all bankrupt or the industry was monopolized. During the 1970s the federal government began to deregulate large parts of the transportation, communications, energy, and financial industries because it became clear that economic regulation was, in fact, impeding competition that could benefit consumers.[8] Today, federal price regulations are largely confined to agricultural commodities and international trade of selected products—neither of which is believed to invoke natural monop-oly considerations.[9]

Agriculture

Economic regulation of agriculture amounts to an array of subsidies, including subsidies for being a farmer, subsidies for not making money on what is grown, and subsidies for taking land out of production. In 2000 government assistance constituted all of the overall farm income in eight states. Generally, subsidies mainly go to Big Agribusiness corporations and the richest farmers. The Environmental Working Group reported that in 2003 the top 6 percent of recipients collected 55 percent of all subsidies. Although subsidies used to be inversely related to farm prices (that is, they would increase when farm prices fell), that relationship has not been true in recent years. For example, according to the U.S. Department of Agri-culture, farm earnings in 2004 reached a record $74 billion, while direct

8. Of course, political factors played an important role in deregulation. It should also be noted that most formerly regulated industries are not completely deregulated, especially telecommunications and electricity. I discuss the effects of partial deregulation of these industries later.

9. Some local governments control the price of selected rental housing. Early (1999) and Glaeser and Luttmer (2003) analyze the effect of rent control in New York City on rents and the quality of housing. The minimum wage is another form of price regulation, but it is intended in principle to con-tribute to the social goal of reducing poverty by raising the earnings of the working poor rather than to correct a market failure. As pointed out in footnote 3, monopsony power is rarely a factor in low wage rates.

government payments were as high as they were in years when farmers earned much less.

Historically, government intervention in agriculture was motivated by the "farm problem"—that is, the low earnings of most farmers and the great instability of income from farming. But as reported by Gardner (1992), careful estimates indicate a convergence of farm and nonfarm incomes in the late 1960s and average farm incomes exceeding average nonfarm incomes by the 1980s. Farm and nonfarm labor markets have become much more integrated, with some family members living on a farm and commuting to nonfarm jobs while other family members work on the farm. On average, farmers have also become wealthier than non-farmers. The core of the farm problem is therefore rejected by basic data. Yet, governmental assistance to agriculture continues and has even accelerated in recent years.

Price support programs for certain agricultural commodities were initially created under the 1933 Agricultural Adjustment Act, which has been revised every few years since its inception. Currently, commodities such as wheat, corn, cotton, peanuts, dairy products, sugar, and rice are eligible for price supports. (Long-standing tobacco price supports ended as of the 2004 crop year.) The agricultural sector also idles much of its land as part of the Department of Agriculture's acreage reduction authority. Prices for fluid milk and milk used in dairy products are set by the federal government in accordance with the Milk Marketing Order of 1937. This program effectively raises the price of fluid milk and lowers the price of manufactured dairy products (Helmberger and Chen 1994).

Government regulation (subsidization) of these markets cannot be justified on economic grounds; thus, commodity price support programs basically amount to transfers from consumers to producers that generate annual net welfare losses of $3.0 billion to $12.4 billion (Rausser 1992; Robinson, Kilkenny, and Adelman 1989). The dairy support program also generates welfare losses that approach $1 billion a year (Helmberger and Chen 1994). The 1996 Federal Agricultural Improvement and Reform Act attempted to scale back the costs of the programs (including their restrictions on planting) and to eventually wean farmers from taxpayer support, but Congress yielded to pleas from farmers and their lobbyists and provided annual "emergency" loans that raised the program's costs. In May

2003, President George W. Bush signed a ten-year $190 billion farm sub-sidy bill that, among other things, increased payments to farmers who pro-duce wheat and corn and introduced a new $1.3 billion milk price support program.

International Trade

Instead of benefiting from direct subsidies, certain industries have bene-fited from the federal government's system of quotas and tariffs that restrict the availability of foreign competitors' automobiles and light trucks, steel, textiles and apparel, chemicals, dairy products, and sugar. (Beginning in 1981 domestic sugar producers also received price supports.) Protection for an "infant industry" could be justified for a limited time. Tariffs could also be justified if they increased national welfare at the expense of foreign firms without starting a trade war. However, a large volume of empirical evi-dence indicates that trade protection has mainly generated gains to estab-lished U.S. industries that fall far short of the losses to consumers. Feenstra (1992) draws on several studies and puts the annual net cost to the United States of tariffs and quotas between $12 billion and $18 billion. To add insult to injury, import prices are raised by the 1920 Jones Act, which increases the cost of transporting imported goods by requiring that coastal shipping be on U.S.-built and U.S.-owned vessels.[10]

Notwithstanding these costs, the United States and its trading partners have gradually reduced trade restrictions outside of agriculture by binding policy to multilateral agreements. But political considerations still result in the imposition of tariffs and quotas for certain products at almost any time. Upon taking office, President Bush expressed a desire to end all tariffs on consumer goods, but he then supported new tariffs of 8–30 percent on a broad range of steel products imported from Japan, South Korea, Taiwan, China, Russia, and Europe. Bush subsequently lifted the tariffs but indi-cated that he could impose them again. Quotas on textiles and apparels

10. International competition of airline service has been regulated through bilateral agreements that provide the framework under which fares and service frequency between the United States and other countries are determined. Morrison and Winston (1995) estimate that fares between the United States and foreign destinations would, on average, decline 25 percent if they were determined in an environ-ment that paralleled deregulated competition on U.S. domestic routes.

around the world ended on December 31, 2004. However, the Bush administration reacted to a flood of Chinese clothing imports since January 2005 by announcing it would impose new quotas on cotton shirts, trousers, and underwear from China. The United States and China have subsequently negotiated a trade agreement that limits China's clothing exports for the next three years.

4 | Social Regulation: Imperfect Information and Externalities

Competitive markets are an essential step toward efficient resource allocation, but efficiency also requires that buyers and sellers be fully informed and that their actions do not affect the welfare of others. Market participants can adjust their behavior to reduce the social cost of imperfect information and of consumption and production externalities, but information and externality policies may raise social welfare further. In theory, these so-called *social regulations* seek to protect public health, safety, and the environment by encouraging consumers and producers to take account of the effect of their actions on others' utility.[1] In practice, the economic policy issue is to determine the most efficient way to compel socially desirable behavior.

Imperfect Information

If consumers are uninformed or misinformed about the quality of a product, they may derive less utility from it than they expected. Consumers'

---

1. The liability system administered by the courts also, in theory, seeks to reduce the cost of externalities by encouraging firms and consumers to behave in a more socially efficient manner. The Economics of Liability Symposium in the Summer 1991 *Journal of Economic Perspectives* provides an overview of the system.

choices could be distorted by false advertising, by firms' failures to disclose relevant information about their products and services, and by a lack of information to assess accurately the safety of potentially risky products. Similarly, workers may become injured or ill because they lack information about the health risks they may encounter in their workplace.

The federal government attempts to minimize the welfare losses caused by imperfect information by empowering regulatory agencies to direct firms to provide complete and accurate information about their products and workplaces and to ensure that consumer products and workplaces meet reasonable safety standards.

Descriptive data suggest that the incidence of illnesses and injuries caused by certain products has stabilized and that workplace injuries are a declining problem in the United States. Unsafe drugs cause adverse reactions in patients leading to serious illness or death. Although it is quite difficult to separate drug safety from doctor or patient error, to control for the mix of drugs over time, and to determine whether adverse drug reactions pose a serious health risk, a meta-analysis of several studies by Lazarou, Pomeranz, and Corey (1998) indicates that the incidence of adverse drug reactions among hospitalized patients has remained stable over the last thirty years. In a similar vein, although changes in sampling methodology and the relative popularity of different products make it difficult to track the evolution of injuries associated with particular product categories, there is no evidence that a systematic change in injuries has occurred over the past thirty years. Finally, the number of occupational injuries has steadily declined for the past three decades in private industry (figure 4-1a) and in mining (figure 4-1b). (It is unlikely that the recent spike in mining accidents in 2006 signifies a change in the long-run trend.)

Are government regulations or market forces responsible for these types of favorable trends? Or is there simply not much of a problem in the first place? The summary findings that I draw from the current state of the available scholarly evidence are:

Potential information problems in product markets and workplaces have not led to significant welfare losses to the public. Government actions generally amount to weak solutions in search of a problem because the policies implemented to date have not provided much social benefit.

Figure 4-1a. *Occupational Injuries for Private Industry, 1973–2001*[a]

Injuries

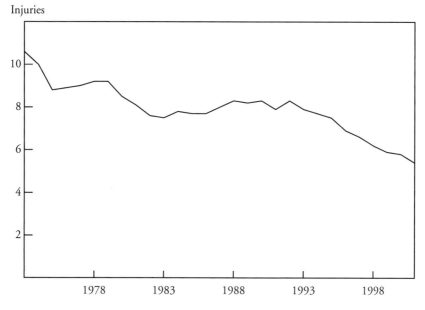

Source: U.S. Department of Labor, Bureau of Labor Statistics, statistics on workplace injuries, illnesses, and fatalities.

a. Rate of occupational injuries are per 100 full-time workers and include all injuries sustained on the job, including those that require time off from work and those that do not.

Advertising Regulation

Since the 1910s, the Federal Trade Commission has sought to promote truth in advertising. Specifically, it is responsible for preventing deceptive acts or practices in the sale of various products, with particular attention given to food, drugs, and alcohol. In accordance with its regulations that define deceptive practices, the FTC conducts investigations of alleged false advertising and can order firms to stop running particular ads.

Peltzman (1981) found that the investigations raised firms' costs, but it was unclear whether they enabled consumers to make more informed choices that enhanced their welfare. Mathios and Plummer (1989) concluded that the FTC's action to prohibit Wonder Bread's nutritional claims was unnecessary because the messages that were challenged lacked materiality for consumers and, in fact, were discontinued. Ringold and Calfee (1990) pointed out that FTC advertising regulation may actually

Figure 4-1b. *Occupational Injuries for the Mining Industry, 1976–2002*[a]

Injuries

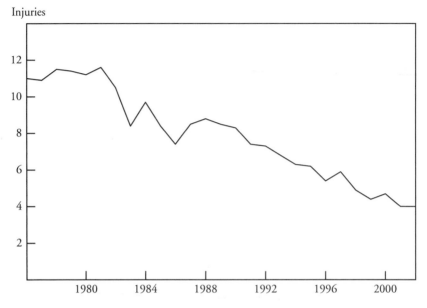

Source: U.S. Department of Labor, Mine Safety and Health Administration, workplace injury, illness, and fatality statistics.

a. Rate of occupational injuries are per 100 full-time workers.

limit the availability of potentially useful consumer information. Specifically, they argued that the agency's cigarette advertising regulations prohibited sellers of less harmful cigarettes from making claims that raised valid health concerns, thereby hindering the introduction and sale of safer products.

Studies disagree about whether FTC actions have produced much benefit to consumers. Sauer and Leffler (1990) concluded that the FTC's Advertising Substantiation Program, developed in the early 1970s, along with changes in the legal definition of deception, probably made advertising more credible. But the authors used very indirect measures of the credibility of advertising such as changes in how much firms advertise certain products. Calfee and Ringold (1994) focused on surveys of consumers' attitudes toward advertising. Analyzing six decades of data that began in the 1930s, they found for each decade that 70 percent of consumers thought that advertising was often untruthful and sought to persuade people to buy things they did not want. (Nonetheless, consumers also believed that advertising provided useful information.) The authors argued that the stability of consumers' beliefs about advertising through time—especially during the 1970s when advertising regulation moved from extreme laxity to unprecedented force and the 1980s when regulation receded—was inconsistent with the view that advertising regulation increased the credibility of advertising. Such results are hardly conclusive, but they raise doubts about whether FTC advertising regulation has enabled consumers to make more informed choices.

Disclosure

Federal laws and agencies also require certain sellers to provide all relevant information that might affect whether people choose their products and services. Instead of requiring automakers to report information about the safety performance of their vehicles, the National Highway and Traffic Safety Administration makes the results of automobile crash tests directly available to the public. Economists have not done extensive empirical work in this area, but they have explored whether policies requiring disclosure of information have aided investors, air travelers, and motorists.

The 1933 Truth-in-Securities Act requires an issuer of securities worth more than $300,000 to file a statement for potential investors that contains material facts such as the firm's capital structure. However, the information required by the law did not appear to go beyond the information required by the New York Stock Exchange (NYSE). Indeed, the NYSE signaled investment quality by its decisions on which securities to list. Jarrell (1981) analyzed stock returns before and after the law was implemented and found that it provided few benefits to investors. Simon (1989) found that the law did not affect mean returns at the NYSE, although returns were somewhat higher for initial public offerings in other (regional) stock exchanges. Simon also found that the variance of returns was reduced for some issues of stock, but she argued that the Securities Act may have produced costs by shifting riskier over-the-counter securities to lower-cost, unregulated markets.[2]

2. The 1964 Securities Act Amendments extended mandatory disclosure regulations to large firms traded over the counter. Greenstone, Oyer, and Vissing-Jorgensen (2006) found that shareholders valued the disclosure requirements. But the authors cautioned that they could not conclude that the amendments had a positive welfare effect because they could not rule out the possibility that shareholders' gains were offset by managers' losses.

More recent equity market regulations potentially affecting investors include the Williams Act of 1968, which regulated corporate takeovers by requiring a bidder to disclose certain facts and figures and by instituting a minimum tender period, and the Sarbanes-Oxley Act of 2002, which specified new standards for corporate governance. The Williams Act was intended to protect target firms' shareholders by providing them with more information about the acquiring firm and by giving them more time to decide whether to tender. Jarrell and Bradley (1980) concluded that shareholders of target firms were better off because the Williams Act increased cash tender premiums. But the authors also noted that the higher premiums created substantial social costs by deterring some takeovers that would have improved economic efficiency and by harming shareholders of firms that would have been acquired absent the takeover laws. Surveying the relevant empirical accounting and finance literature, Romano (2005) argued that the corporate governance provisions in the Sarbanes-Oxley Act were ill conceived. Evidence on the actual social costs and benefits of that law must await future research.

Computer Reservation Systems (CRSs) have been used by travel agents to book flights for travelers. The now defunct Civil Aeronautics Board and Congress took steps to prevent owners of CRSs, usually a carrier or group of carriers, from displaying information in a manner that favored one airline over its competitors. Morrison and Winston (1995) found that efforts to eliminate CRS bias had little effect on air travelers' welfare because most fliers did not rely on information from a CRS to determine their preferred flight or were loyal to a specific frequent flier program and insisted on getting flight information about their regular carrier.

NHTSA has tried to inform automobile consumers by making the results of automobile crash tests available to the public. Hoffer, Pruitt, and Reilly (1992) argued that consumers paid little attention to the government's information and relied on other sources of safety performance such as trade publications. Apparently, this was a wise choice because the authors found that NHTSA's crash test data were a poor predictor of vehicle safety. The data have been recently questioned for failing to account for the different effects that accidents between large sport utility vehicles and smaller cars have on their occupants and for the dangers posed by rollover crashes involving SUVs.

Labeling

As noted in the case of FTC cigarette advertising regulation, some sellers have an incentive to disclose potentially useful information when product quality (safety) varies. Until the mid-1980s, manufacturers were prohibited by law from promoting the health content of their food products through advertising. When the prohibition was lifted, the consumption of fiber cereals increased and the consumption of fat and saturated fat decreased (Ippolito and Mathios 1990, 1995). Moreover, advertising was an important source of information that affected consumer behavior.

The 1990 Nutrition Labeling and Education Act (NLEA) tried to improve on market behavior by requiring most manufacturers of food products to include nutrition information on labels and by authorizing the Food and Drug Administration to regulate health claims. Mathios (2000) assessed the effect of the NLEA on the salad dressing market. He found that salad dressings with little or no fat voluntarily disclosed health information, but that the law eliminated differences in disclosure among, and modestly shifted demand from, brands with more fat. But the earlier findings of Ippolito and Mathios suggest that any beneficial effects of the 1990 law could have been achieved by informative advertising in the absence of the NLEA. Indeed, the FDA has recently attempted to increase the role of competition in improving the health consequences of a food product by issuing rules that give producers more leeway to make health claims about their products than they had under the 1990 law.[3] While it is not clear that it intends to make particular health claims, in 2006 the McDonald's fast-food chain will voluntarily use packaging for its food products that lists nutritional data including calorie, fat, and sodium levels.

Eco-labeling may promote environmental objectives. Perhaps the most notorious case involves dolphins, which have been used by fishermen as a way of finding and netting tuna. During the late 1980s consumers became aware that the harvest of yellowfin tuna caused the incidental mortality of dolphins. Media attention eventually spurred calls for consumer boycotts of canned tuna. In April 1990 the three largest tuna canners in the United

---

3. This information is contained in Department of Health and Human Services, Food and Drug Administration, "Guidance for Industry: Qualified Health Claims in the Labeling of Conventional Foods and Dietary Supplements," *Federal Register*, December 20, 2002.

States announced a policy of labeling their tuna as dolphin safe, and other canners quickly followed. The federal government responded by passing the Dolphin Protection Consumer Information Act of 1990, which mandates that tuna products cannot be labeled as "dolphin safe" unless dolphins were not used to capture tuna for the entire fishing trip, as verified by a sanctioned observer aboard the boat.

Teisl, Roe, and Hicks (2002) found that consumers reacted positively to dolphin-safe labels because the market share for canned tuna increased. But given that firms recognize that consumers have a preference for dolphin-safe tuna, one could argue that eco-labeling was driven by market forces rather than government policy. Indeed, it is not clear that the 1990 law had much effect on the accuracy of labeling. At the same time, the legislation may have verified the authenticity of tuna sellers' claims in the minds of the public.

Viscusi and Magat (1987) offered evidence that people behave in a rational manner in response to risk by updating their assessments of it and by either taking greater precautions in the case of consumer products or demanding higher wages for jobs that pose greater risks to health. Hazard warning labels are therefore a potentially useful source of information about risks to health. Firms have long provided these labels on various products, and government policy has required labels on cigarette packages, hazardous chemicals, and similar dangerous products. Unfortunately, it has been difficult to assess the costs and benefits of actual policies requiring warning labels because they are often inextricably associated with media attention that has focused on the potential harm from the hazard (for example, the 1964 surgeon general's report on smoking). In any case, Magat and Viscusi (1992) suggested that information policies such as hazard warning labels are likely to be far more effective in promoting safety than government campaigns that try to persuade people to change their behavior.[4]

Standards

When products such as home appliances, drugs, and automobiles are used improperly or have design flaws (or, in the case of drugs, unintended side

4. For example, Blomquist (1988) concluded that federal campaigns to increase seat-belt use were largely ineffective.

effects), they may pose health hazards that are not understood by consumers. Federal agencies have tried to reduce risks to consumer safety by setting standards to ensure that products are not flawed when they appear on the market and, in the case of drugs, verifying that they pose minimal risks to consumers before they appear on the market.

The Consumer Product Safety Commission (CPSC) has broad authority to set standards to eliminate what it perceives to be unreasonable risks to consumer safety from products normally found in the home. It can also issue bans and recalls of products that it deems to be unacceptably dangerous. Grabowski and Vernon (1978) and Viscusi (1985) analyzed the effect of CPSC regulations on the home accident rate and found that they had a statistically insignificant effect. It appears that the regulations were ineffective because they addressed only a small aspect of a product and bore only a tangential relationship to product safety. In addition, Thomas (1988) conducted a case study of the CPSC and found that its preferences among projects caused it to misallocate resources and create systematic "bureaucratic failure." Specifically, the commission tended to select projects with potentially large benefits but low benefit-cost ratios.

New drugs hold the promise to reduce pain and suffering and to prolong life for millions of people, but they may also compromise a patient's health if they turn out to have harmful side effects. In accordance with the 1962 Drug Amendments, the FDA provides premarket approval of all new drug claims to reduce health risks. It also must approve new drugs before they can be offered for sale. Naturally, the approval process delays the introduction of new drugs. The economic issues are whether the FDA imposes excessive delays and whether the process reduces the risks from using new drugs.[5]

Peltzman (1973), Grabowski (1980), and Wiggins (1981) concluded that FDA policies were excessively cautious and reduced the flow of new drugs on the market. Drugs eventually approved for sale in the United States were delayed by several years compared with the same drugs sold, for example, in Great Britain. These delays amounted to a 5–10 percent tax on annual drug purchases during the 1970s and 1980s and undoubtedly cost thousands of lives. Of course, FDA regulations may have kept harmful

---

5. In theory, the liability system also provides pharmaceutical companies with an incentive to reduce the risk from new drugs. Empirical evidence on the liability system's effect on drug safety is not available.

drugs from appearing on the market and therefore saved many lives. Unfortunately, researchers have yet to quantify these potentially important benefits.

The costs of the delays were reflected in increasing complaints by pharmaceutical firms, AIDS activists, and other patient groups. Government's response was the 1992 Prescription Drug User Fee Act, which required pharmaceutical firms to pay fees to the FDA so the agency could hire new-drug reviewers in the Center for Drug Evaluation and Research to improve the speed and efficiency of reviews. The program, subject to renewal every five years, has specific performance targets that the FDA must seek to achieve, such as a six-month review for the most therapeutically novel drugs and a ten-month target for less novel drugs. Olson (2002) and Philipson and others (2005) found that the introduction of user fees reduced new-drug review times and increased the flow of new drugs on the market. For example, between 1985 and 1992 the FDA approved a total of 170 new molecular entities, compared with 259 approved entities from 1993 to 2000. Although the costs of the FDA's review process have been reduced, even the remaining costs cannot be justified until the benefits from FDA evaluations are accurately determined.[6]

The FDA also mandates that patients obtain a prescription from a physician before they can purchase certain potentially harmful drugs. On its face, the law discourages self-treatment in favor of professional treatment, which may benefit patients by reducing the expected toxicity cost of drug consumption. But Peltzman (1987) pointed out that the prescription requirement may give patients a false sense of safety and induce them to consume stronger medicine to obtain the benefits of more aggressive treatment. His empirical estimates indicate that the prescription requirement has not reduced but, in fact, may have increased poisonings from overdoses. (It has also failed to reduce infectious disease mortality rates.) Peltz-

6. Between 1998 and 2001 ten drugs were withdrawn from the market for safety reasons. Recently, Merck pulled Vioxx and Pfizer pulled Bextra off the market. These actions appear to have prompted the FDA to be more cautious in its reviews, thus reducing the flow of drugs on to the market and again raising the question whether the cautious reviews are justified on cost-benefit grounds. Indeed, drugs approved in the first half of 2005 took almost twice as long to win approval as drugs approved during the same period in 2004. The FDA also placed five times as many black-box warnings—the agency's most serious alert—in the first half of 2005 than it had in the first half of 2004. Although no controls are made for the different mix of drugs in these periods, it appears that the FDA is slowing down its process out of political rather than medical concerns.

man's finding illustrates how regulation may create an "offset effect"—that is, consumers are induced to engage in risky behavior such as shifting consumption to more powerful drugs with less certain effects in response to policies that are intended to improve safety.

Offsetting behavior has also occurred in response to National Highway and Traffic Safety Administration automobile safety regulations. In the late 1960s NHTSA required automobiles to be equipped with seat belts and other safety features such as padded dashboards. Peltzman (1975) found that the overall benefits to travelers' health from these regulations as reflected in fewer fatalities and injuries were completely offset by drivers taking more risks (such as driving faster, running red lights, and so on) that increased pedestrian deaths and nonfatal accidents. (Certain drivers did gain utility from the greater mobility associated with driving faster.) Subsequent research has debated the magnitude of the offset effect (see, for example, Crandall and others 1986), but few researchers question its existence.[7]

Workers may face health hazards at their workplaces because facilities and equipment are improperly maintained, conditions are dangerous, and so on. The Occupational Safety and Health Administration (OSHA) is empowered to reduce risk in the workplace by setting safety standards, conducting inspections to see that workplaces conform to them, and assessing penalties on employers who do not. OSHA's sister agency, the Mine Safety and Health Administration (MSHA), performs these tasks for mines.

Figure 4-1a shows that the rate of occupational injuries in private industry has declined since the early 1970s, but OSHA's contribution to the decline is questionable. Schultze (1977) criticized OSHA because it failed to address the greatest influence on the injury rate, the employee turnover rate (this influence was reported by Oi 1974), and instead focused on easily identifiable and correctable hazards that could be addressed effectively by the market (that is, companies have to pay employees higher wages, or

7. Offsetting behavior has been found to occur in response to other changes in the driving environment such as mandatory seat-belt laws, repeal of the national 55-mile-per-hour speed limit, and the widespread adoption of airbags and antilock brakes (Winston, Maheshri, and Mannering 2006). It is also notable that findings of offsetting behavior have been obtained using very different methodologies, ranging from time series analysis of automobile fatalities data aggregated at the national level to structural models of drivers' choices of automobile safety devices and accident outcomes estimated on disaggregated data.

compensating differentials, to work in hazardous conditions) and workers' compensation. Workers' compensation, which requires employers to purchase insurance to compensate workers if they are injured at work, is designed to reduce the litigation costs that would arise if workers could sue their employers for job-related injuries. The system provides a powerful incentive for employers to maintain safe workplaces because workers' compensation insurance rates are tied to a firm's injury experience (accident performance). Moore and Viscusi (1990) estimate that in the absence of workers' compensation, job fatality rates in the United States would be as much as one-third greater than they are.

Considerable empirical evidence, including time series studies by Bartel and Thomas (1985), Viscusi (1986), and Smith (1992) and simulations by Kniesner and Leeth (1999), indicates OSHA regulations and enforcement have had a modest effect, at best, and often a statistically insignificant effect on the workplace accident rate. Gray and Scholz (1993) contended that researchers have tended to underestimate OSHA's impact on safety, but their quantitative estimates are actually quite similar to Viscusi's.[8] Finally, Weil (1996) found that OSHA inspections of plants in the custom woodworking industry influence plants to comply with machine-guarding standards. But he failed to find a strong link between the inspections and lost days of work, which implies that the standards are not targeting the causes of the most serious injuries. As noted, workers' compensation and market forces—and in all likelihood increasing societal wealth—have contributed to improvements in workplace safety. OSHA's ineffectiveness appears to be explained by poorly designed safety standards, weak enforcement, and a lack of a significant safety problem at most workplaces.[9] Accordingly, the social desirability of OSHA's activity is clearly in question.

8. The two studies obtain similar estimates—only about 2–3 percent of workplace injuries are prevented by OSHA enforcement—despite using very different methodologies. Viscusi uses industry-level data and estimates a basic time series model, while Gray and Scholz use plant-level data and control for unobserved heterogeneity, serial correlation, and endogeneity.

9. A recent proposal to improve OSHA's effectiveness would increase the maximum criminal penalty from six months to ten years for employers who cause the death of a worker by willfully violating workplace safety laws. Stiffer criminal penalties, however, may not compensate for ineffective safety standards and weak enforcement. For example, during the1980s and 1990s OSHA investigated more than 1,200 cases where investigators concluded that workers died because of their employers' "willful" safety violations but prosecuted a mere 7 percent of these cases.

Notwithstanding the long-term decline in coal mine fatalities shown in figure 4-1b, recent tragedies in three mines have raised concerns about whether the Mine Safety and Health Administration needs to strengthen enforcement of mine safety standards. Industry observers assert that growing mechanization of equipment has contributed to mine safety and that MSHA's role has been minimal because fines for safety violations are small, negotiable, and often not even collected.

Sider's (1983) assessment of mine safety attributed reductions in fatalities per man-hour to improvements in productivity rather than to changes in mining operations induced by regulation. Similar to workers in other occupations that face significant risks to their health from inherent working conditions, miners have received wage premiums to compensate them for the risks they take by working in mines, such as breathing harmful air matter, suffering injuries, or even dying if a mine collapses. Thus mine owners have a strong financial incentive to prevent wage premiums from rising by keeping their mines safe and preventing accidents that increase the perceived risks to health from working in a mine.

Kniesner and Leeth (2004) estimated that the costs of MSHA's activities are more than double the benefits. Its budget is large—on a per establishment basis, it is 400 times larger than OSHA's budget—and its deterrence is weak. MSHA could generate greater social returns by reallocating its funds to ensure that safety violations that contribute the most to injuries are corrected.

Information Policies Adopted by States

Individual states have adopted information policies to supplement federal policies. These include prohibiting price advertising that may divert attention from product quality, requiring practitioners in hundreds of occupations to obtain a license that certifies they are competent to perform a particular task, enabling purchasers of new automobiles to obtain a full refund or a replacement vehicle in the event that their automobile is hopelessly defective, and requiring motor vehicles to have annual safety inspections. Empirical evidence indicates that consumers have not been better served by these policies than by federal policies; in fact, in some instances they have been harmed.

Several states prohibit firms from advertising the prices of particular products and services on the grounds that consumers may be induced to purchase a lower-priced alternative that compromises their health or safety. Yet price advertising may provide information to consumers about product quality and spur competition that weakens the ability of firms to elevate prices above costs. Indeed, economists have found that prohibitions on price and other contents of advertising have raised prices and the variation of prices for eyeglasses (Benham 1972), drugs (Cady 1976), optometric services (Kwoka 1984; Haas-Wilson 1986), and routine legal services (Schroeter, Smith, and Cox 1987) without shielding consumers from products or services that may jeopardize their health.

Occupational licensing is a form of entry regulation that requires individuals to obtain a license if they wish to provide services in sectors such as law, dentistry, engineering, and even hairdressing. States use licensing to regulate more than eight hundred occupations, representing nearly 20 percent of the nation's workers. Licensing may be justified if consumers are likely to be harmed because they are not able or not willing to judge the competence of individuals who provide an important service. But licensing may also have unintended effects such as encouraging do-it-yourself behavior, wasting overtrained talent, and reducing the quantity of available workers. Carroll and Gaston (1981) argued that by reducing the quantity of available workers, occupational licensing may reduce the quality of services and consumer safety. They presented suggestive evidence that this outcome occurred in several occupations, including electricians (that is, fewer electricians were associated with more accidental deaths by electric shock from nonindustrial activity), dentists, plumbers, and so on. Kleiner and Kudrle (2000) concluded that occupational licensing did not raise the quality of service consumers received. In the case of dentistry, they found that consumer costs increased in states with more stringent licensing but that dental health did not improve and malpractice suits did not decrease.

U.S. and foreign automobile manufacturers have vastly improved the quality of their vehicles during the past few decades. Nonetheless, it is possible that some consumers may purchase a "lemon" because they are not able to detect serious defects in the vehicle until they have driven it for a while (Akerlof 1970). Lemon laws give consumers who have purchased a hopelessly defective vehicle an opportunity, typically for one year, to request either a full refund or a replacement vehicle from the manufacturer. Of course, the market also provides quality insurance against defective vehicles, such as Chrysler's buyback plan that allowed consumers to return their new car for a full refund within thirty days of purchase. Smithson and Thomas (1988) found that lemon laws are rarely utilized because they do not significantly improve upon market remedies and may involve significant transactions costs (for example, consumers are required to engage first in arbitration with a dealer before they can proceed with litigation). Some recent evidence indicates the difficulties in actually trying to receive compensation under various state lemon laws. It is estimated that of the small fraction of consumers who contest defective vehicles in arbitration, only about 10 percent prevail.[10]

Even if their vehicles are not lemons, motorists may not be aware that aging vehicles can pose safety risks; thus, roughly twenty states mandate that all registered vehicles have safety inspections to detect and correct mechanical problems. Vehicle inspections would be expected to improve highway safety by forcing motorists to retire their vehicles earlier than they would have in the absence of inspections or by increasing expenditures on repairs. But Poitras and Sutter (2002) found that vehicle inspections have not had either of these effects, which casts doubt on whether they have improved highway safety.

I have not found any direct evidence that consumers have been substantially informed, protected, or insured by federal or state information policies. However, an assessment of information policy is not complete without considering whether these policies have benefited consumers by deterring harmful products from being produced and keeping them off the market. As indicated previously, deterrence can have opposing effects: FDA drug evaluations, for example, may have kept harmful drugs off the market and saved lives but may have also delayed potentially helpful drugs from appearing on the market for decades—even beyond the well-documented approval lag. Policy recommendations on how to improve FDA drug evaluations and other information policies would be enriched by research that quantifies and sorts out the benefits and costs of their deterrence effects.

10. Don Oldenburg, "Recourse for When That Sweet Ride Turns Sour," *Washington Post*, February 26, 2006, p. F5.

Externalities

Externalities are positive or negative spillovers caused by an agent's action that affect the welfare of others. Government can increase efficiency by using pricing or quantity policies to make consumers and firms account for the social costs (or enable them to accrue the social benefits) of their actions. Quantity policies take the form of *commands* (specific limits are set for a particular externality such as air pollution) or *controls* (specific technologies are required to abate an externality), or both. Recently policy-makers have explored market-oriented approaches, such as emissions trading programs, to reduce externality costs more efficiently.

Research and development by private firms may generate positive externalities for competitors, thereby resulting in a suboptimal level of innovative activity because firms cannot fully appropriate the benefits of their R&D. Government policy has tried to spur innovative activity by subsidizing firms' R&D and providing patent protection.

In contrast to alleged market power abuses or imperfect information, externalities have caused serious social problems justifying government intervention. And government policy has in some cases made progress in curbing social costs. High ambient levels of air pollutants in the 1960s have declined noticeably following the 1970 Clean Air Act (figure 4-2). Similarly, a dwindling percentage of the U.S. population has been exposed to aircraft noise following federal action (figure 4-3). At the same time, the quality of the nation's water bodies has failed to improve in the past few decades (figure 4-4).[11]

The basic research question motivated by these stylized facts is whether government policy has generated significant net benefits in the process of reducing the social cost of externalities. The summary findings that I draw from the current state of the available scholarly evidence are:

Some policies have been expensive successes because although their benefits have exceeded costs, the gains could have been achieved at much lower cost. Others have been outright failures because their

---

11. The definitions of different water qualities were not formalized until 1986. The percent of all water bodies sampled has increased over time, although coastlines are sampled less often than are other bodies of water.

Figure 4-2. *Average Ambient Levels of Air Pollutants, 1965–1995*[a]

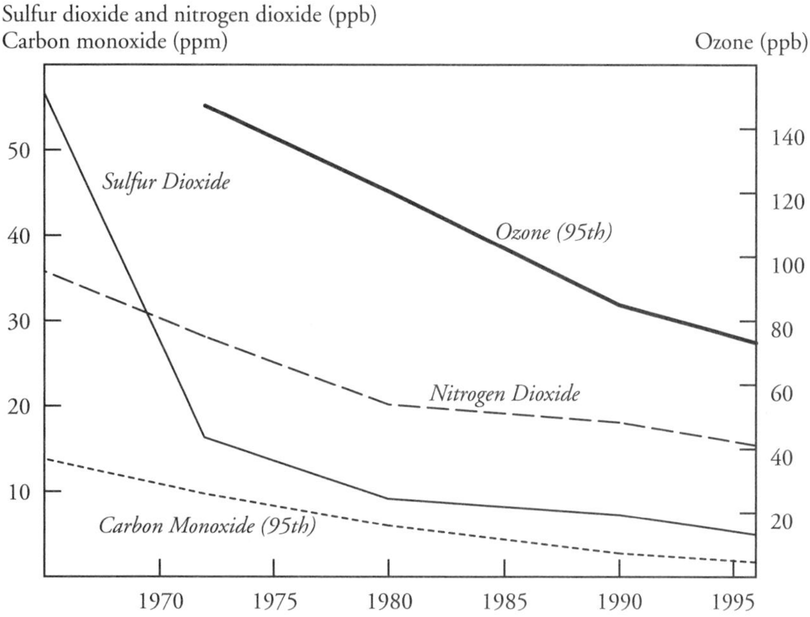

Sulfur dioxide and nitrogen dioxide (ppb)
Carbon monoxide (ppm)   Ozone (ppb)

Source: Based on data reported in Lipfert and Morris (2002).
ppb = parts per billion; ppm = parts per million.
a. Carbon monoxide and ozone levels are averages of the 95th percentile of daily one-hour readings at each monitoring location. Sulfur dioxide and nitrogen dioxide levels are averages of annual means from each monitoring location.

costs have exceeded benefits. In contrast, market-oriented approaches implemented by the government have shown promise of producing large improvements in social welfare by curbing externalities at lower cost than current policies do.

Consumption Externalities

Consumption externalities arise from a consumer's use of a product or service that imposes costs on other individuals and the environment. The most notable externalities include automobile emissions, airplane noise, and overconsumption of health care caused by smoking and drinking. Consumption of energy increases the nation's dependence on foreign oil, which may subject the nation to losses in consumer surplus. Two other

Figure 4-3. *Percentage of Population Exposed to Excessive Aircraft Noise*[a]

Percent

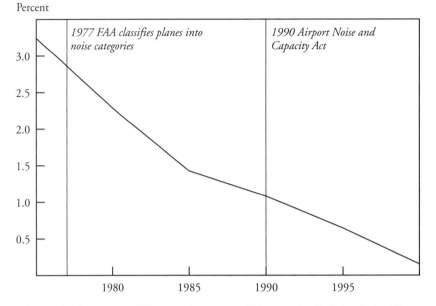

Source: U.S. Department of Transportation, Bureau of Transportation Statistics, *National Transportation Statistics 2002*, Table 4-53.

a. Excessive noise is defined as noise levels of 65dBA (decibels) or higher.

major externalities, highway and airport congestion, will be discussed in the context of financing public enterprises.[12]

Policymakers have preferred to address consumption externalities by using commands to influence the behavior of manufacturers rather than by using prices to influence the behavior of consumers. Schultze (1977) questioned whether commands could be an effective policy instrument on the grounds that government's imagination of how its particular actions can generate social efficiency and its ability to command an appropriate level of performance are not up to the task.

Carbon monoxide, hydrocarbons, and nitrogen oxide motor vehicle emissions damage agriculture, create smog, and cause some individuals to suffer respiratory problems. To reduce these costs, Congress passed the

12. Local communities have established zoning ordinances, which in theory may reduce externalities associated with noise, unsightly buildings, and so on. However, researchers have found that zoning regulations have increased housing prices for both owner-occupied and rental housing and reduced construction of new housing (Glaeser and Gyourko 2003; Quigley and Raphael 2005).

Figure 4-4. *Percentage of Sampled Water Bodies Considered "Impaired" or Worse by the EPA, 1986–2000*

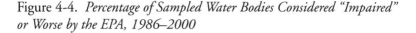

Percent

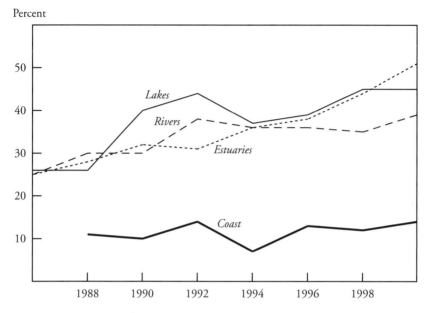

Source: U.S. Environmental Protection Agency, *National Water Quality Inventory Report to Congress* (1986, 1988, 1990, 1992, 1994, 1996, 1998, 2000).

1970 Clean Air Act amendments which set emissions standards for new light-duty vehicles and empowered the Environmental Protection Agency to enforce them.[13] Until recently, airplanes, heavy-duty diesel trucks, and buses have all but escaped the pollution control standards that have been imposed on new cars and light trucks.

The 1970 amendments have been associated with the dramatic decline in emissions shown in figure 4-2 (Crandall and others 1986). Agriculture has benefited from smog reductions, but researchers have found it difficult to link emissions reductions with improvements in the health of residents in metropolitan areas. At the same time, Crandall and others estimated that the new emissions-related technology spurred by the Clean Air Act raised the cost of a new car nearly $1,000 in the mid-1980s.

13. Federal emissions standards also existed before 1970. The standards contained in the 1970 act affected nonstationary as well as stationary sources of emissions.

Although it is not clear whether the benefits from reduced emissions exceed the costs, it is clear that a given level of benefits could have been obtained at lower costs. It would have been much more efficient to impose an emissions tax that would have been paid by drivers of all (new and used) vehicles, thus reducing emissions and raising fuel economy because more motorists would have been inclined to shift to new vehicles or to drive their old vehicles less. With the development of remote emissions-detection systems, which have been tested in a number of cities since the mid-1990s, it is still possible to implement such a tax. Instead, the EPA has continued to enforce various regulations such as those driven by the Clean Air Act Amendments of 1990 that include standards for cold temperature carbon monoxide, onboard refueling, and vapor recovery among others. The costs and benefits of these policies have not been assessed, but at this point the net benefits from further reductions in vehicle pollution appear to be small.[14]

Beginning in the early 1970s, the Federal Aviation Administration (FAA) set noise standards for aircraft designs (based on maximum allowable decibel levels) to reduce noise for people who live, work, or pursue recreational activities close to airports. The reduction in noise would be expected to increase property values in the surrounding area. Airlines could either replace their planes that did not meet the noise standards with planes that did or retrofit their planes with "hush kits" so that they complied with the standards. Morrison, Winston, and Watson (1999) estimated that the FAA design standards effectively shortened the life of airlines' capital stock. The increased costs to airlines turned out to exceed the benefits to homeowners, as reflected in higher property values, by $5 billion (present discounted value). An optimal airplane noise tax would have generated only $0.2 billion in net benefits (present value), suggesting that airplane noise has not imposed significant social costs.

Smoking and excessive drinking raise health care costs and life insurance premiums for all members of society.[15] In addition, second-hand smoke may be harmful to nonsmokers. Smokers and drinkers pay federal and state taxes for cigarettes and alcohol that are justifiable as externality taxes. Researchers

14. Concerns about global warming are motivating some states to adopt emissions standards that are tougher than current federal standards. States are able to do this if they adopt California's regulations. California has special authority to set its own air quality rules because it did so before passage of the federal Clean Air Act.

15. The externalities associated with smoking and drinking would be considerably less if health insurance rates were established according to accurate experience ratings.

agree that the tax levels are inefficient, but they have not reached a consensus about whether the taxes are above or below optimal levels that would appropriately charge smokers and drinkers for their consumption of health care services and their higher probability of premature death.

Grossman and others (1993) concluded that current taxes should be much higher to account fully for the social costs of cigarettes and alcohol, and Gruber and Koszegi (2002) contended that the taxes should be higher to provide a self-control device to offset the time inconsistency of smokers' preferences. Viscusi (2002) disagreed and presented evidence that smokers pay their way—that is, financial costs—when the higher costs associated with their greater medical care, sick leave, group life insurance, fires, and taxes from lost earnings are balanced against the cost savings associated with less nursing home care and forgone retirement and pension benefits due to their shorter life expectancies.[16] Another argument against raising cigarette taxes is that the current level has created a thriving illegal market for cigarettes. Higher taxes may expand activity that has diverted billions of dollars from legitimate businesses and government to criminals and exposed law-abiding citizens, such as truck drivers and clerks, to violent crimes.

Viscusi acknowledged that the costs of second-hand smoke are a legitimate concern but noted that studies did not control for important household characteristics, including but not limited to a spouse who smokes. In any case, he still argued that smokers probably pay their way even accounting for these costs.

The energy crises in the 1970s heightened federal interest in policies that would conserve energy and reduce the nation's dependence on foreign oil. The alleged justification for these policies is that energy consumption creates an externality because it increases the share of (more costly) oil imports. Given recent tensions in the Middle East, it has also been argued that it is not in America's interest to import oil from hostile countries that may use the profits from their exports to fund terrorist activities.

The most significant attempt to conserve energy has been the imposition of Corporate Average Fuel Economy (CAFE) standards.[17] Set in the early 1970s by the U.S. Department of Transportation, CAFE sought to

16. Mukamal and others (2003) found a reduced risk of heart attack among men associated with moderate alcohol consumption.

17. Congress tried to induce motorists to conserve energy by setting a national maximum speed limit of 55 miles per hour, which took effect in 1974. In 1999 Lave and Lave reported that the new

increase the fuel economy of new cars. Its economic effects, however, have been a source of controversy. One view is that it is well-known that consumers value fuel economy, but CAFE has generally failed to influence the two market forces that encourage consumers to purchase fuel-efficient vehicles: gas prices and the profit-maximizing incentives that automakers have to produce such vehicles (Crandall 1992). To the extent that it has increased fuel economy for new vehicles, CAFE has actually encouraged some people to drive more, and by raising vehicle prices the standards have increased emissions because they have encouraged people to retain their used vehicles longer (Kleit 2004; Portney and others 2003).

CAFE has also compromised safety by distorting the mix of large and small vehicles. Crandall and Graham (1989) argued that CAFE caused consumers to shift from large cars to small cars. Eight years later, Godek (1997) found that CAFE caused consumers to shift to light trucks (vans, minivans, and SUVs) instead of small cars and estimated that 50 percent of the increase in the share of light trucks since the 1970s could be attributed to CAFE, thereby offsetting 75 percent of the vehicle weight that would have been lost otherwise. The shift to light trucks increased fuel consumption, and although light trucks increase their occupants' safety, they increase injury severity from a collision to occupants of smaller vehicles and to pedestrians, bicyclists, and motorcyclists. Gayer (2004) provided evidence that operators of light trucks were more likely than operators of a car to be involved in a crash, while White (2004) found that motorist fatalities had increased as a result of the greater share of light trucks on the road.[18] In sum, critics of CAFE doubt that it has contributed much to energy conservation but point out that it has unintentionally generated other social costs.

David Greene has been the most visible researcher offering support for CAFE. In a 1998 paper, he drew on his and others' research to argue that

---

law had a very small effect on fuel consumption but suggested it was retained because of the large improvement in safety that appeared to accompany it. In 1996 the national speed limit was abolished. Contrary to widespread predictions, Lave and Lave showed that fatality rates actually fell following repeal of the limit.

18. A very modest increase in fuel efficiency standards for light trucks was instituted in August 2005. The standard for light trucks must average 24 miles per gallon (mpg) on an industrywide scale by 2011, up from roughly 22 mpg on 2006 models. Fuel efficiency standards were set in March 2006 for the heaviest vehicles in this category such as the Hummer H2 and Ford Excursion. For example, the Hummer H2 will have to increase its mpg from 13.8 to 22 by 2011.

CAFE worked in the sense of reducing fuel consumption, at least in some years. But he did not offer an overall estimate of the net benefits of CAFE, accounting for all the costs noted above, and failed to make a strong case for why CAFE is more efficient than changes in gasoline prices. His concern about prices is that consumers and producers cannot efficiently adjust their behavior to gasoline-price signals. But this concern hardly seems valid, given that owners of trucks, buses, airplanes, and used cars respond to changes in gasoline prices in an expected fashion (Dahl and Sterner, 1991, provided some evidence). Theory suggests it is more efficient to confront transportation operators with higher fuel prices than to rely on CAFE to reduce oil consumption. Proponents of CAFE have yet to mount a serious challenge to the theory.

The National Appliance Energy Conservation Act of 1987 set national energy efficiency standards for major appliances. Sutherland (1991) pointed out that the standards raised consumers' initial capital costs and lowered operating costs for these appliances, but he found no evidence that this trade-off improved on the efficiency of appliances that would exist absent the standards. Newell, Jaffe, and Stavins (1999) decomposed the sources of energy efficiency for room air conditioners and gas water heaters and found that increases in energy prices and better technology accounted for most of the improvements; energy efficiency standards appear to have had a small effect.

Production Externalities

Negative production externalities arise when firms impose costs on consumers and the environment by polluting the air and water, creating hazardous wastes, and depleting fishing stocks or other natural resources.[19] As in the case of consumption externalities, the government has tended to use command-and-control policies rather than the price mechanism to encourage behavior that would maximize net benefits and reduce social costs.

---

19. Firms also produce greenhouse gases, which contribute to climate change. I do not, however, assess externality policy in this area. As discussed by Poterba (1993), considerable uncertainty surrounds both the physical and economic consequences of greenhouse gas accumulation. No climate change (global warming) tax currently exists, and it is not clear what—if any—the benefits from an optimal tax would be. This is not to minimize the potential importance of the matter. More evidence is necessary, however, before appropriate policy can be formulated and assessed.

Recently, the government has conducted experiments that replace command-and-control policies with selected "cap-and-trade," or "allowance trading," programs that set a limit on the total amount of pollution that can be emitted from all regulated sources (such as power plants) and allow the sources to buy or sell allowances (that is, an authorization to emit a fixed amount of a pollutant) on the open market (Burtraw and Palmer 2004).

Following the 1970 Clean Air Act amendments, the EPA established a minimum level of air quality that all counties are required to meet for four pollutants: carbon monoxide, tropospheric ozone, sulfur dioxide, and total suspended particulates. Every county in the United States receives attainment or nonattainment status for each pollutant. Emitters of regulated pollutants in nonattainment counties are subject to stricter EPA oversight than emitters in attainment counties. The EPA sets specific rates of emission for each pollution source and requires specific technologies to abate a given pollution source, or in the case of sulfur dioxide allows firms to bid in the open market for pollution allowances (tradable permits).

Estimates of the welfare effects of pollution command-and-control regulations have tended to vary widely, with the most reasonable point estimate suggesting small net benefits because the significant benefits from cleaner air, including higher property values and improved health, have been offset by the high costs imposed on U.S. industry (Portney 1990; Hazilla and Kopp 1990). In addition, polluting industries have limited the benefits from pollution controls by moving from nonattainment counties to attainment counties (Henderson 1996).[20] Some recent studies also have found both high benefits and high costs of the Clean Air Act, although it is difficult to combine them to obtain an aggregate estimate of net benefits. Benefits during the late 1970s include a reduction in infant mortality valued at as much as $11 billion and an increase in property values of roughly $45 billion (Chay and Greenstone 2001, 2005). In contrast, during 1972–87 nonattainment counties lost some $75 billion in output in pollution-intensive industries (Greenstone 2002).

---

20. As part of the Clean Air Act, the New Source Review requirements stipulate that when an existing plant seeks to modify its operations, the entire plant must comply with current standards for sources of pollution. However, List, Millimet, and McHone (2004) find that these requirements retard plant modification rates and do little to accelerate the closure of dirty plants. Recent regulations under the Clean Air Act allow plant operators to modernize their operations without installing expensive new pollution control equipment, but these rules have been challenged in court.

In 1990 the Environmental Protection Agency set up a trading system in which power companies could buy and sell allowances to emit sulfur dioxide. A company could choose whether it was more cost effective to install scrubbers to reduce sulfur dioxide emissions or to buy allowances from a firm that emits less pollution. Each year the number of these allowances has dropped, with the goal of cutting SO_2 emissions in half by 2012. Tradable permits have generated noticeable welfare improvements over EPA regulations. For example, holding pollution standards constant, sulfur dioxide emissions trading has reduced firms' abatement costs 25–34 percent compared with command-and-control policies (Schmalensee and others 1998; Carlson and others 2000). Annual savings amount to $700 million–$800 million.

The federal government also deserves credit for introducing market-oriented approaches to reduce other sources of pollution. The marketable lead permit system that was used to phase out leaded gasoline in the United States was highly cost effective, saving hundreds of millions of dollars (Hahn and Hester 1989).[21] Flexible trading programs have also been initiated to reduce nitrogen oxide (NO_x) emissions in the electricity sector. Burtraw, Bharvirkar, and McGuinness (2003) showed that additional benefits could be achieved by expanding summertime NO_x programs to the full year. The EPA recently issued a rule to reduce mercury emissions from power plants through a cap-and-trade system that allows some power plants to make deep pollution cuts while others make none.

Another potentially effective policy to reduce pollution is the EPA's Toxic Release Inventory Program (TRI). Created as part of the Superfund reform legislation in 1986, the program requires facilities that handle threshold amounts of specific chemicals to provide annual reports to the EPA of their releases of these toxic substances and where they end up. TRI is effectively an information policy that seeks to influence plants to reduce their emissions by exposing the pollution levels they have created. However, it does not expose levels of toxicity or environmental damage. Hamilton (2005) summarized some evidence suggesting that TRI has caused plants in certain locales to improve their environmental performance, but noted that the benefits are difficult to quantify because publicly available

21. Caps and emissions permits have also been used to reduce chlorofluorocarbons (CFCs) around the world.

pollution data for most of the pollutants covered by TRI were not available before the start of the program. Further research is needed to verify the accuracy of the data that plants are required to report, the costs and benefits of plants' compliance with the program, and whether the program could be improved by requiring additional information.

Water quality became a mainly federal responsibility with the passage of the Water Pollution Control Act Amendments of 1972. The EPA establishes command-and-control regulations for major water pollutants. Estimates of the welfare effects of these regulations tend to have a wide range, with the most reasonable point estimates suggesting that the benefits fall substantially short of abatement costs (Portney 1990; Hazilla and Kopp 1990). It also appears that the EPA undermines potential benefits by its lax enforcement. For example, during 1999–2001 the EPA imposed fines on less than 7 percent of firms that committed violations. It seems unlikely that such a low level of punishment is justified by a cost-benefit analysis of the EPA's enforcement policy. As in the case of air pollution, efficient effluent charges including permits could significantly raise net benefits by reducing producers' costs.

The 1980 Comprehensive Environmental Response, Compensation, and Liability Act, which became known as the Superfund program, was created to clean up hazardous wastes from a variety of industrial sources. The act gave the EPA the right to initiate remedial cleanups at sites where a release or significant threat of a release of a hazardous substance posed an imminent and substantial danger to public welfare and the environment. A trust fund supported by special taxes on chemical and petroleum corporations and administered by the EPA was used to clean up contamination at so-called orphan sites (those where the responsible party could not be identified or could not pay), as well as at sites requiring emergency action or facing resistance from recalcitrant offenders. Contaminated sites pose health risks to exposed residents, most notably a greater chance of cancer. The industry taxes that initially fed Superfund were discontinued in 1995 and have been replaced by taxpayer revenues.

Hamilton and Viscusi (1999) concluded that regardless of where its funding came from, Superfund failed to allocate its resources to the environmental problems posing the greatest social costs. For example, 95 percent of expenditures were used for projects that eliminated only 0.5 percent of the cancer risk at those waste sites. The median cost per life saved,

$388 million, is two orders of magnitude above conventional estimates of the value of life (Viscusi 1993; Viscusi and Aldy 2003). By choosing more cost-effective cleanups, the EPA could safeguard the health of more residents who are potentially at risk from hazardous wastes and incur lower expenditures.

Superfund's cost effectiveness has also been assessed through its impact on homebuyers' willingness to pay (WTP) for remediated residential property. Gayer, Hamilton, and Viscusi (2000) estimated that the cost of the EPA's remediation plan at Superfund sites in the greater Grand Rapids, Michigan, area greatly exceeded residents' WTP for the reduction in risk at these sites. Greenstone and Gallagher (2005) also found that the average WTP by consumers of housing services in affected areas was considerably below the mean cost of a Superfund cleanup.

Competitive commercial fishermen could substantially deplete the stock of certain fish in open waters if there were no restrictions on harvesting. Thus, federal and state policies have attempted to promote fishery conservation by instituting various regulations that limit the length of the fishing season, the number of boats in a particular area, and total seasonal catch. Adler (2005) noted that none of the policies had worked particularly well because fishermen seek to catch as many commercially desirable fish as possible before the season closes. In the process, American fishing operations have discarded the most unwanted fish, amounting in recent years to roughly 20 percent, or more than one million tons, of total fish caught.

Adler reported that the National Marine Fisheries Service acknowledges that out of the 932 fish stocks under federal management, the status of nearly 700 is unknown. Some case studies have found that fishery regulations have been ineffective. Squires and Kirkley (1991) found that sablefish quotas were undermined by offsetting behavior as fishermen discarded or killed a large fraction of their sablefish catch to keep the most commercially desirable fish and still stay within their quotas. Androkovich and Stollery (1989) questioned whether a serious market failure existed in certain markets because even an optimal tax to regulate commercial fishing did not generate significant welfare gains.

Recent market responses have helped to promote conservation of fish stocks. For example, harvests for an assortment of fish have been sustained at high levels because fleets have sought ever more distant fish populations and reduced the incidence of wasteful discards and unintentional kills. In addition, fish farms now account for more than 40 percent of the fish that the United States imports. Thus, although yearly quotas on red grouper in the Gulf of Mexico were reached in October 2005, restaurants around the country were able to serve grouper from fish farms in Asia. Market-oriented policies have also been helpful. For example, similar to allowance-trading programs, dedicated access privileges programs allocate shares of a fishery to individual fishermen, who can buy and sell shares. In Alaska, fishermen are granted a portion of the allowed halibut catch and trade these quotas among themselves to make more efficient use of the available stock. Current holders can also sell or lease quotas to new entrants. Leal (2006) reported several benefits from this system: fishermen have been able to sell fresh Pacific halibut by staggering their catches over a longer fishing season; safety has improved because fishermen have more flexibility on which days to fish; and fewer fish have been wasted and discarded.

Innovation

In contrast to the preceding negative externalities, innovative activity by firms may create positive spillovers to their actual or potential competitors. Innovative effort may therefore be suboptimal, creating a form of market failure, because knowledge can be transmitted (either copied or imitated) from its creator to prospective competitors at low cost. The federal government has tried to spur innovation by subsidizing firms and by establishing the patent system so firms and universities can appropriate some of the positive spillovers from their R&D. The subsidies include direct funding, tax credits, and competitions. Some federally funded R&D is contracted out to universities or companies but undertaken at federal facilities such as Los Alamos National Laboratory or the National Institutes of Health. A patent gives a firm or an individual the exclusive use of an invention for a certain period of time.

Klette, Moen, and Griliches (2000) cast strong doubt on whether federal programs have supported socially beneficial programs that would not have been undertaken without federal assistance. According to Hall (1996), federally funded R&D generated low social returns and did little to encourage private R&D spending. Indeed, Wallsten (2000) obtained evidence based on the Small Business Innovation Research Program suggesting that public sector subsidies may significantly crowd out private funding. Federal support of large commercial projects such as light-water nuclear reactors, breeder reactors, and synthetic fuels ended in failure (Cohen and Noll 1991). In 1993 the Clinton administration initiated the "Partnership for a New Generation of Vehicles" with domestic automakers in hopes of producing a high-gas-mileage car using a hybrid propulsion system by the decade's end. At a cost to taxpayers of $1.5 billion, the goal was never accomplished. Ironically, the two automakers that began offering hybrid vehicles to American consumers in the 1990s, Honda and Toyota, received none of the subsidy.[22]

The federal government also undertakes R&D at federal laboratories and public agencies such as NASA. Although I have been unable to find academic assessments of the welfare effects and justification for this activity, the efficiency of NASA's endeavors has been called into question by the media. For example, the Space Shuttle program has averaged about five trips a year at a cost of at least $500 million per launch with little scientific advance to show for the public's outlays. The X-33, a re-useable launching vehicle that would fly frequently, reduce the cost of sending cargo into space, and improve safety, was expected to replace the Shuttle. NASA cancelled the project after investing nearly $1 billion in it.[23]

R&D tax credits and competitions do stimulate additional private R&D spending (Lichtenberg 1988; Mamuneas and Nadiri 1996), but they do not substantially close the gap between private and social returns. Moreover, Jaffe (2002) argued that assessments of these programs suffer from a serious selectivity problem because funding often goes to firms and industries that are likely to be innovative without public money.

With the possible exception of Milton Friedman, economists tend to believe that academic research, much of which is funded by the federal government, generates high social rates of return and is therefore worthy of more support than it has received to date. Mansfield (1991) estimated that the annual social rate of return from university research in the late 1970s approached 30 percent. Jaffe (1989) found that university research increased commercial innovation as indicated by greater corporate patenting in the areas of drugs and medical technology, and electronics, optics,

22. George F. McClure, "Are We on the Road to Energy Independence?" *Today's Engineer* (IEEE), February-March 2002.

23. Warren E. Leary, "NASA Ends Project Intended to Replace Shuttle," *New York Times*, March 2, 2001.

and nuclear technology. Generally, certain industries are able to benefit from scholarly research because universities have less incentive than firms to keep research secret. Kim, Lee, and Marschke (2005) argued that university research stimulates innovative activity of firms in the pharmaceutical and semiconductor industries because such firms tend to employ and collaborate with researchers who have worked in university laboratories. As potential inventors accumulate more experience in conducting university research, patents in these industries increase.

The patent system seeks to establish property rights in an activity that may otherwise suffer from the market failure of nonexclusivity (an innovation generates positive spillovers to competitors) and nonappropriability (an innovator is unable to fully capture profits from an innovation). An optimal patent policy maximizes the difference between the social benefits from innovations and the sum of the deadweight costs from conferring a monopoly position on the inventor, the costs of preempting other firms' activities (which may lead to inefficient efforts to get around a patent), and the transactions costs of granting patents, including litigation costs. Inventors may claim a patent by applying to the U.S. Patent and Trademark Office. The patent office is responsible for ensuring that the invention is clearly specified, nonobvious, novel, and useful and covers patentable subject matter. High-quality patents also enable those "skilled in the art" to comprehend, use, and eventually build upon the invention. Low-quality patents are vague and may discourage would-be innovators because they fear legal action for patent infringement. Litigation also arises when the patent office reexamines a patent at the urging of a third party.

Patent law was standardized across the country by the 1982 Federal Courts Improvement Act, which required judicial appeals of patent cases to be handled by a single, specialized appeals court, rather than the twelve regional courts of appeal, as had previously been the case. In addition, the costs of the patent office itself were paid by the patent applicants. Jaffe and Lerner (2004) argued that although there was no empirical basis for changing the patent system, the new court of appeals has interpreted patent law to make it easier to get patents, easier to enforce patents against others, easier to get large financial awards from such enforcement, and harder for those accused of infringing patents to challenge the patents' validity. These changes have led to explosive growth both in patent applications and awards (figure 4-5a) and in patent suits (figure 4-5b) since the early 1980s.

Figure 4-5a. *Annual Patent Applications and Awards, 1840–2003*

Thousands

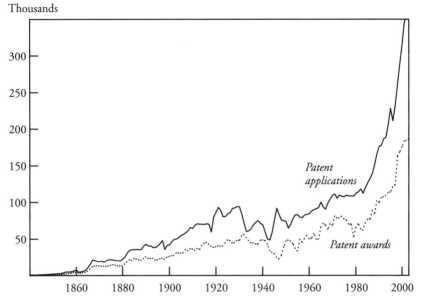

Source: U.S. Patent and Trademark Office.

Given that the litigation cost of a patent infringement suit may run into the tens of millions of dollars, it is clear that strengthening patent protection has increased the transactions costs associated with the system. In addition, patent protection could hinder R&D. For example, rapid progress in a technology such as semiconductors may have been stymied by strong intellectual property protection (Levin and others 1987). Today, software developers are potentially constrained by patent laws. In fact, a survey by Burton (1996) indicated that nearly 80 percent of software programmers thought that software patent law impeded software development, compared with less than 10 percent of programmers who thought the law promoted development. Even IBM has recognized the problem and has released 500 of its software patents for free use as part of the open source initiative to stimulate further computational innovations.

Turning to the system's benefits, economists have long questioned whether patent protection of any strength provides a strong incentive for firms to invest in R&D (Mansfield 1986; Mazzoleni and Nelson 1998; Jaffe 2000). To the extent that patents may have increased innovative activity, it

Figure 4-5b. *Annual Number of Patent Lawsuits Initiated, 1946–2003*

Number

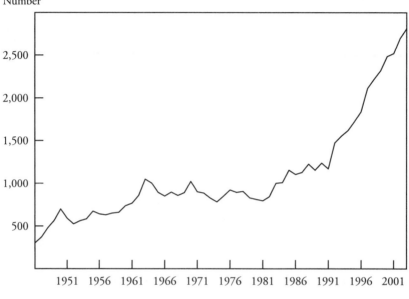

Source: Jaffe and Lerner (2004).

appears to be confined to the pharmaceutical and biotechnology areas and possibly specialty chemicals (Cohen and Levin 1989; Hall 2003). In any case, the limited evidence available casts doubt on the patent system's efficiency and in light of responses to the 1982 legislation raises questions about whether the system is raising or lowering social welfare.

Uncertainty about the overall welfare effects of the patent system means that to some extent there is no "base case" to assess comprehensive policy reforms that may improve the system and enhance its contribution to social welfare. However, the Congressional Budget Office (1998) assessed the effect of a change in patent terms in a specific industry that was part of a socially beneficial policy. The 1984 Drug Price Competition and Patent Term Restoration Act (also known as the Hatch-Waxman Act) attempted to improve competition in the pharmaceutical industry while still providing incentives for innovation. The act extended patent terms for innovator (branded) drugs by three years, on average, and greatly expedited the approval process for generic prescription drugs so that the average time between the expiration of a brand name drug's patent and entry by a generic drug was reduced from more than three years to less than three months. In particular, manufacturers of generic drugs no longer had to meet duplicative testing requirements to obtain FDA approval.

Today, nearly all branded drugs face intense competition from generic drugs once their patent expires. The Congressional Budget Office estimated that by facilitating entry of generic drugs, the Hatch-Waxman Act enabled consumers to substitute these drugs for branded drugs and save as much as $12 billion. At the same time, overall investment in drug development appears to have increased since the act. These findings suggest that industry-specific changes in patent policy, perhaps accompanied by other policy reforms, may be an effective approach until appropriate comprehensive reforms can be identified.

5

Public Production

A private firm will provide a good or service if it can earn a normal profit. Market failure occurs when a socially desirable service (that is, one whose social benefits exceed social costs) is not privately offered because it is unprofitable. Market failure also occurs when a service is undersupplied because it is a public good and susceptible to the free rider problem. A pure public good—defense and fresh air are probably the only examples—is nonrivalrous (nobody's consumption lowers anybody else's benefits) and nonexcludable (it is infeasible to prevent those who do not pay for the good from obtaining benefits). Most publicly supplied services are mixed or "impure" public goods such as roads—consumption is rivalrous during congested periods but exclusion may be difficult.

The government can increase social welfare by financing socially desirable services, including public goods, which would not be supplied by the private sector. In practice, the government can provide the service or negotiate a contract with a private firm to provide the service. In any case, the government can maximize social welfare by setting efficient user charges for public facilities and by financing investments in the facilities that equate marginal benefits and marginal costs.[1] The facilities requiring the largest investments constitute the nation's physical infrastructure.

1. Efficient user charges amount to marginal cost pricing. If production is characterized by large scale economies, then efficiency calls for marginal cost pricing with subsidy because marginal costs are below average costs. If no subsidies are available, efficiency calls for Ramsey prices, where the percentage markup

61

The federal government, sometimes in collaboration with state and local governments, is responsible for financing and managing highways, airports, air traffic control, inland waterways, public land, urban transit, intercity passenger rail, and mail services.[2] As noted, the theoretical rationale for public financing of major infrastructure and certain services is that the private sector would find it unprofitable to do so. In general, economists have not tried to determine whether private production is feasible and, if so, whether it would generate greater net benefits than public production. Instead, researchers have taken federal, state, and local government control over more than $1 trillion of the nation's physical capital as given and investigated whether pricing, investment, and operating policies are maximizing economic welfare. Of course, the public sector may fall short of allocating resources in accordance with optimal pricing and investment policies but nonetheless improve on what the private sector's provision, if any, would have been. However, growing concerns with the waste associated with public financing of important social services is raising questions about whether such provision is better than allowing the private sector to finance and offer these services.[3]

Descriptive measures indicate that some of the nation's public infrastructure and services are beset with economic problems. The speed and reliability of automobile travel has been increasingly compromised by congestion and delays in major metropolitan areas (figure 5-1); delays in air travel that were temporarily curtailed by the September 11 terrorist attacks are as great as ever (figure 5-2); and public transit's operating deficits are a growing drain on the public purse (figure 5-3) during a period when its patronage has declined. Transit's total deficits are even greater than shown because it also receives substantial capital subsidies. The summary findings that I draw from the current state of the available scholarly evidence are:

of prices above marginal costs is inversely related to users' demand elasticities subject to a break-even constraint. Empirical work indicates that marginal cost pricing without subsidy is a feasible benchmark for the facilities and services assessed here.

2. Government is also responsible for building and maintaining dams and sewers and for public water and power agencies. I am not aware of recent scholarly economic assessments of government's provision of this infrastructure. Schultze (1977) discusses the cost inefficiencies associated with federal grants to aid construction of municipal waste treatment plants.

3. Government has used market mechanisms to allocate some public goods such as the electromagnetic spectrum. I discuss these experiments later.

Figure 5-1. *Average Annual Traffic Delay in Major Metropolitan Areas,*
1982–2001

Hours per person

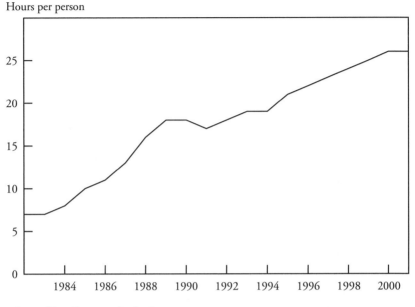

Source: Texas Transportation Institute.

Public financing and management of transportation infrastructure,
public lands, and various services have been extremely inefficient and
have strained the budgets of all levels of government.

Transportation Infrastructure and Public Lands

Federal, state, and local governments are responsible for building, maintaining, and rehabilitating U.S. highways. Valued at more than $1 trillion,
the nation's road system is its largest civilian investment, according to the
Bureau of Economic Analysis. Highway expenditures are primarily financed by state and federal gasoline taxes. These taxes are also generally the
only "price" that vehicles must pay for using the road system. State and federal governments hire private contractors to undertake various road projects such as rehabilitation and major construction. In accordance with the

Figure 5-2. *Changes in Air Travel Time, 1977–2004*

Minutes

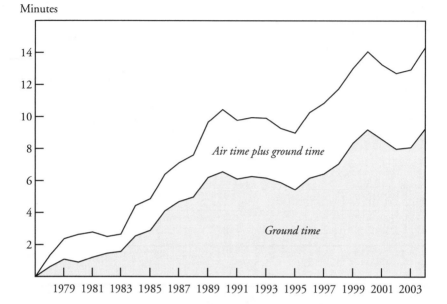

Source: U.S. Department of Transportation, Service Segment Data and Schedule T-100, Data Bank 28DS, Domestic Segment Data.

Davis-Bacon Act, these contractors must be paid union wages that are applicable to the jurisdiction where the work takes place.

Public management of roads is characterized by substantial pricing, investment, and production inefficiencies (these issues are discussed in Small, Winston, and Evans 1989). Roads are built to a given capacity (lane miles) to accommodate cars and trucks, and to a given durability (pavement thickness) to accommodate heavy trucks. All vehicles contribute to congestion, which occurs mainly during peak commuting periods when the ratio of traffic volume to capacity exceeds a certain threshold, forcing vehicles to travel at less than free-flow speeds allowed by law. Heavy trucks increase the frequency that road pavement must be resurfaced; pavement wear itself is related to roughly the third power of a truck's weight per axle. Given these considerations, gasoline taxes are an inefficient pricing mechanism because they are basically invariant to changes in traffic volume throughout the day and are *inversely* related to a truck's weight per axle

Figure 5-3. *Government Transit Operating Assistance, 1976–2001*

Billions of dollars (2001)

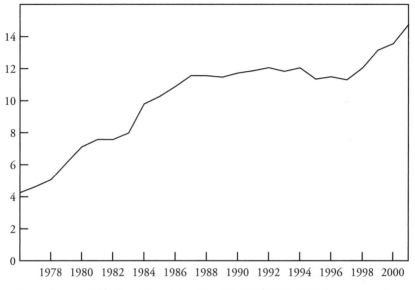

Source: American Public Transit Association, *Transit Fact Book* (1992, 1998) (www.apta.com).

(that is, trucks with more axles that reduce pavement damage get lower fuel economy and pay higher gasoline taxes).

Investments in highway durability must trade off the maintenance costs of current pavement against the capital costs of building thicker pavement; optimal investments minimize the sum of these costs. Generally, highway authorities have failed to minimize investment costs because they have preferred to build thinner pavements to reduce the up-front capital costs. Consequently, all roads, from local thoroughfares to major interstates, experience excessive maintenance costs because they must be repaved sooner than if they were built to optimal (thicker) standards. In addition, the speed and reliability of highway transportation have been adversely affected by the growing share of freeways and arterials in fair or worse condition over the past twenty years.

Highway spending has also been used to expand highway capacity and repair roads in well-traveled areas to reduce congestion. But Winston and Langer (2006) found that, on average, one dollar of spending in a given year reduces the congestion costs to road users by only eleven cents in that year and only a few cents in subsequent years. The efficacy of highway expenditures is compromised by the lack of an explicit mechanism that links such spending with congestion in specific localities. But the most fundamental obstacle to highway spending that could efficiently reduce congestion is that the U.S. road system is largely complete and the nation's urbanized areas have little available land to expand their infrastructure.

Finally, highway production costs are inflated by bureaucratic rules that make it difficult to use the latest and most efficient production technologies and by Davis-Bacon constraints that prevent highway authorities from hiring and paying workers who would be willing to work for lower wages than the prevailing union rate.

Small, Winston, and Evans (1989) estimated that replacing gasoline taxes with marginal cost congestion tolls and pavement-wear taxes and building roads to optimal pavement thickness would generate an annual welfare gain of $23.9 billion. Congestion tolls that vary by time of day and location would reduce delays and make efficient use of scarce road capacity. In addition, efficient highway tolls, which reduce excessive driving during peak periods, would justify a substantial reduction in (inefficient) highway expenditures. Such tolls can also be adjusted to account for possible political objections to reducing the welfare of low-income motorists, who place less value on travel time savings than high-income motorists do, without sacrificing much of the gains in efficiency (Small, Winston, and Yan 2006). Marginal cost pavement-wear taxes that are based on a truck's weight per axle and vary by road type would encourage truckers to shift to vehicles with more axles that do less damage to the roads.

Improving highway production efficiency would significantly add to these gains. For example, Kessler and Katz (2001) estimate that the Davis-Bacon Act costs the federal government some $1.5 billion annually. This figure does not simply represent a transfer to labor because no market failure is being corrected, while inflated wages must be financed by additional tax revenues, which creates an additional inefficiency.

Responsibility for designing and operating airports lies primarily with local governments. Airport expenses are covered by passenger facility charges and landing fees, which are set by local airport authorities based on an aircraft's weight subject to guidelines set by the Federal Aviation Administration. Airports that seek federal assistance for investments, such as building a new runway or lengthening an existing one, must receive FAA approval and satisfy the EPA's environmental impact review.

Congestion at a given airport varies by time of day in accordance with the volume of aircraft traffic. Aircraft weight has little effect on congestion because a plane waiting to take off or land is delayed roughly the same amount of time by a jumbo jet as by a small private plane; thus, weight-based landing fees bear little relationship to airport congestion. Runway construction and expansion face formidable political and bureaucratic obstacles, as indicated by the five- to ten-year average delay to add runway capacity. Unfortunately, the FAA has done little to expedite the review process. Indeed, since the mid-1990s only a handful of new runways have been put into service at the most congested airports. Morrison and Winston (1989) estimated that replacing weight-based landing fees with marginal cost takeoff and landing tolls and adding runways at congested airports to maximize net benefits would generate an annual welfare gain of $18 billion. As in the case of highway pricing, airport congestion tolls that vary by location and time of day would make efficient use of scarce runway capacity.[4]

The U.S. air traffic control system monitors domestic airspace to ensure safety and reduce delay. The FAA is responsible for hiring air traffic control personnel and for supplying facilities with new equipment. The FAA has been sharply criticized by commercial airlines and Congress for its tardiness in procuring and implementing up-to-date technology that could expand runway and airspace capacity. In addition, Morrison and Winston (2005) argued that political influences cause the FAA to allocate its resources inefficiently. They found that a reallocation of FAA expenditures toward airports that experience the greatest delays would generate more than $1 billion in annual time savings to air travelers and cost savings to airlines.

Inland waterways are used by water freight carriers to transport bulk commodities and low-value goods. The Bureau of Reclamation and the Army Corps of Engineers are responsible for building and rehabilitating the waterways. In 1952 Senator Paul Douglas, an economist by profession,

---

4. Recent research implies that the benefits of congestion pricing at airports dominated by a single commercial airline carrier are smaller than believed because the hub-dominant carrier internalizes congestion that it causes itself and because a hubbing carrier does not operate at the same times of day as nonhubbing carriers do (Brueckner 2002; Mayer and Sinai 2003). Morrison and Winston (2005), however, found that these considerations, while valid, only modestly reduce benefits from congestion pricing because the bulk of the welfare cost of delays is attributable to operations by commercial and commuter carriers and general aviation that do not internalize delay.

pointed out that waterway projects were often fundamentally flawed on economic grounds because the Corps tended to overstate benefits and greatly underestimate costs.

To the best of my knowledge, scholars have not recently assessed the social desirability of waterway projects, but such projects have attracted considerable media scrutiny because of wasteful investments attributable to powerful political interests. For example, after the Corps was forced to delay its seven-year study of major construction projects on the Mississippi River because an independent economic assessment determined that the study's forecasts of barge traffic were inflated, Senator Christopher Bond of Missouri vowed to make sure that projects were funded no matter what the economic studies concluded.[5]

Beginning with a series of articles that ran in 2000 in the *Washington Post*, Michael Grunwald has reported the most egregious examples of the Army Corps' inefficiencies. Although this information does not constitute scholarly evidence, it may someday provide grist for an academic mill. In any case, the inefficiencies that Grunwald identified include consultants' estimates that benefit-cost ratios of recent Army Corps' projects are consistently and unequivocally below one, documentation that the Corps has adjusted cost-benefit calculations to justify projects on the Mississippi and Illinois rivers, and well-founded concerns that the Corps' management of an $8 billion effort to resuscitate the Florida everglades—the largest environmental project in world history—will be plagued by substantial cost overruns. Mounting criticism inside and outside of the Bush administration forced the Corps to suspend work on some 150 congressionally approved water projects in 2002 to review the economic analysis the Corps used to justify them. Not only do most waterway projects have questionable social desirability, but barge companies are charged only a small fraction of the costs of operating, maintaining, and renovating the system.[6]

Finally, federal and state governments are responsible for allocating and managing land for grazing, natural conservation, and recreational activities.

5. Michael Grunwald, "Army Corps Delays Study over Flawed Forecasts," *Washington Post*, October 5, 2000, p. A33.
6. Michael Grunwald, "Corps' Taming of Waterways Doesn't Pay Off," *Washington Post*, January 9, 2000, p. A1. Grunwald recently discussed the Corps' failure to protect New Orleans from Hurricane Katrina, despite spending more in Louisiana than in any other state; see "A Flood of Bad Projects," *Washington Post*, May 14, 2006, p. B1.

The U.S. Department of the Interior also sells parcels of public lands to the private sector. It is not known whether the extent of public land holdings reflects an optimal allocation between the public and private sector, but anecdotal evidence periodically appears in the press charging that the government has sold land to private parties at below-market value. For example, a developer acquired land in Nevada that the Interior's Bureau of Land Management valued at $763,000 and sold it the next day for $4.6 million.[7]

Gardner (1997) provided evidence that the rental prices for all users of public lands were below marginal costs. Grazing fees paid by farmers covered only $15 million–$30 million of the roughly $230 million cost of administering the grazing program, and revenues generated from wood and paper manufacturers that use national forests were well below the costs of reforestation and the opportunity cost of land sales. Users of public land for recreational purposes paid a nominal or zero price that does not cover maintenance costs. In fact, a law passed in 2005 increased the share of sites operated by the National Forest Service that are free of charge.

Optimal management of national forests calls for a careful combination of thinning, prescribed burnings, and fire suppression that allows forests to regenerate without producing fires that cause fatalities and damage residential property. Federal spending on the National Forest Service has grown substantially in the past few decades, but the evidence does not indicate that the increased expenditures have led to improved forest regeneration and public safety. The scientific community argues that healthy forest growth could be achieved more efficiently and safely if the service spent less money and let certain types of fires burn and extinguish naturally (O'Toole 2002). Indeed, the longstanding government policy of putting out fires as quickly as possible has led to excessive biomass in the understory that makes fires more deadly and difficult—and thus more costly—to extinguish.

Services

State and local governments are responsible for managing and providing most of the bus and rail transit in U.S. metropolitan areas. Transit operations

---

7. Joel Brinkley, "A U.S. Agency Is Accused of Collusion in Land Deals," *New York Times*, October 12, 2002, p. 16.

and investments are funded by farebox revenues and federal, state, and local subsidies. Transit pricing, service, and production sharply deviate from standard economic efficiency guidelines. Transit fares are significantly below the marginal cost of transit service and have failed to keep up with rising operating and capital costs. The operating and capital subsidies that make up this shortfall currently approach $20 billion (Winston 2000). Service frequency is excessive; rail fills only 18 percent of its seats with paying passengers throughout the day, and transit buses fill only 14 percent (loads are somewhat higher during the morning and evening rush hours). Transit costs are inflated by oversized vehicles, excessive labor expenses, and low productivity.[8]

Winston and Shirley (1998) estimated that replacing current transit fares with marginal cost fares and providing service frequency to maximize net benefits would produce annual efficiency gains of $9.2 billion. (Accounting for environmental and safety externalities associated with urban travel had little effect on the findings.) Improvements in production efficiency would significantly increase these gains. Recent work by Winston and Maheshri (2006a) assessed whether urban rail transit was actually socially desirable by comparing recent estimates of its social benefits with its subsidies. The authors found that with the single exception of BART in the San Francisco Bay area, every U.S. transit system actually reduced social welfare. Moreover, they could not identify an efficient pricing policy or physical restructuring of the rail network that would enhance any system's social desirability without effectively eliminating its service. Under public management, rail transit has been unable to attract sufficient patronage to reduce its high average costs—a problem that has been complicated enormously by new patterns of urban development with geographically dispersed residences and jobs.

The growth of automobile and airline travel made intercity rail passenger service highly unprofitable by the 1960s, prompting the formation of the National Railroad Passenger Corporation (popularly known as Am-

---

8. Despite their low load factor, sixty-seat buses are used in many urban areas on all routes at all times of day. Regarding labor inefficiencies, Section 13(c) of the 1964 Federal Transit Act makes it prohibitively expensive to release a transit employee by obligating federally supported transit agencies to provide any dismissed employee with a monthly compensation package equal to his or her average monthly earnings during the past twelve months. This compensation must be paid for a period equal to the duration of the employee's employment with the transit agency, capped at *six years*.

trak) in 1970 because private railroads no longer wanted to provide this service. Amtrak is a quasi-public enterprise—that is, it is a corporation without private equity holders. The Amtrak board, which includes the secretary of the U.S. Department of Transportation, must approve any notable fare changes, and Amtrak must maintain its service to a city unless it gives the state (and normally Congress) 180 days notice. Amtrak was expected to be self-sufficient within a few years of its inception and to operate without subsidies. However, it has relied on operating and capital subsidies to continue operations. Recently, subsidies have made up 20–30 percent of its revenues.

Morrison (1990) estimated that Amtrak's overall social benefits were roughly equal to its social costs, a finding that justifies federal subsidies. But he also concluded that its social benefits were highly localized—the gains in the well-traveled Northeast corridor offset the losses in the rest of the United States. Because intercity passenger rail service is not socially desirable in many parts of the country, reductions in it would increase economic efficiency.

Finally, the United States Postal Service is the nation's largest public enterprise, with current annual revenues approaching $70 billion. Reorganized in 1970, it is obligated to provide service for different classes of mail to all U.S. residents. The postal service sets prices with regulatory oversight from the Postal Rate Commission and retains a monopoly in letter delivery. Nearly 80 percent of its expenses are labor related, with wages set through collective bargaining with binding arbitration (Geddes 2005). Except for some senior management positions, postal workers' wages have been estimated to be about 30 percent more than those of comparable private sector workers (Hirsch, Wachter, and Gillula 1999).

The postal system was intended to be financially self-sufficient, but its recent annual losses amount to more than $1 billion. Of greater concern is the falling volume of letter mail, in large part because people have substituted Internet-based communications; as a result postal system deficits were expected to grow to several billion dollars by the end of this decade. Prices for first class mail are above marginal costs and are used to partly subsidize prices for second-, third-, and fourth-class mail, which are below marginal costs (Wattles 1973; Adie 1989; Geddes 2003). The postal service also faces strong political pressures to keep open unneeded mail distribution centers

and underutilized post offices and to use outdated, labor-intensive technologies that not only inflate costs but result in slower mail delivery times
than optimal. In growing recognition that private sector delivery services
could improve its operations, the postal service has recently contracted with
Federal Express and United Parcel Service for assistance in sorting and
transporting mail. A more comprehensive policy of privatization is discussed
later.

6

Policies to Correct Market Failures: Synthesis and Assessment

Economic theory identifies many situations where a market failure may arise and suggests how the government could correct the failure and improve economic efficiency. In practice, potential market failures such as market power and imperfect information do not appear to create large efficiency losses to the U.S. economy. However, market failures arising from externalities such as air and water pollution, hazardous wastes, and traffic congestion do impose significant social costs that government policy could reduce efficiently.

Based on the assessments discussed here and summarized in table 6-1, government policy to correct market failures is characterized by two major flaws—that is, government failures—that cost the U.S. economy hundreds of billions of dollars a year. First, government policy has created economic inefficiencies where significant market failures do not appear to exist, such as with antitrust laws and economic regulations that have raised firms' costs and generated economic rents for various interest groups at the expense of consumer welfare. To be sure, antitrust enforcement may be deterring anticompetitive behavior, especially collusion, but this potentially important benefit has not been verified empirically. Information policies have also raised consumer prices and firms' costs. A possible benefit of this intervention is that some products, such as harmful drugs, may have been prevented from appearing on the market, but

73

Table 6-1. *Welfare Costs of Market Failure Policies*

Policy	Costs
Antitrust	The annual cost to firms that are subject to antitrust investigations and court proceedings from legal expenses and the time and resources expended by management and critical staff to assist in the defense could run into the billions of dollars.
Economic regulation	Annual deadweight losses from commodity price support programs: $3 billion–$12.4 billion. Annual deadweight losses from tariffs and quotas: $12 billion–$18 billion.
Social regulation: imperfect information	FTC investigations of false advertising raise firms' costs. FDA delays of the availability of new drugs have amounted to a 5–10 percent annual tax on drug purchases. OSHA inspections and regulations raise firms' costs. States' prohibitions of advertising raise prices.
Social regulation: externalities	NHTSA-mandated emissions technology raises the price of new vehicles. DOT fuel economy standards raise the price of new vehicles and compromise safety. FAA noise standards raise airlines' costs, exceeding benefits to homeowners by $5 billion (present value). EPA command and control air and water pollution policies raise firms' costs. Superfund's cost-effectiveness is extremely low. Federally funded R&D generates low returns and crowds out private R&D. The current patent system involves large transactions costs.
Public production	Public production runs large deficits that must be covered by taxes that create an excess burden. Annual deadweight losses from inefficient pricing and investment in highways: $23.9 billion. Annual deadweight losses from inefficient pricing and investment in airports: $18 billion. Many inland waterway projects are not cost effective. Users of public land are charged prices below marginal cost. Annual deadweight losses from inefficient pricing and service in public transit: $9.2 billion. Amtrak is not socially desirable in many parts of the country; thus, its subsidy is excessive. Prices for mail service generate inefficient cross subsidies.

once again a potentially important benefit must be confirmed by empirical evidence.[1]

Second, in situations where market failures do exist, government policy has either achieved expensive successes by correcting these failures in a way that sacrifices substantial net benefits or in some cases has actually reduced social welfare. Government policy has wasted resources with its application of command-and-control policies to correct externalities, particularly in health, safety, and environmental policy. Efficient pollution taxes and more extensive use of tradable permits could have reduced automobile emissions, airplane noise, and air and water pollution at much lower cost than current policies. More efficient use of Superfund could reduce the health risks from hazardous wastes for more residents at lower cost. While it is difficult in practice to determine optimal incentives for private R&D, the available research strongly questions whether the socially beneficial innovative activity that can be attributed to publicly supported R&D subsidies and the patent system exceeds the cost of these incentive mechanisms.

Finally, researchers have not determined whether public financing of transportation infrastructure and other services generates greater welfare than would privatization of these activities. But the evidence clearly indicates that public sector pricing, investment, and production policies have failed to ameliorate externalities such as highway and airport congestion, have produced inefficient levels of service, and have resulted in large subsidies that must be financed by general taxes, which in turn create additional inefficiencies—namely, the cost of raising public funds.

What explains the prevalence of government failure when policymakers are presumably trying to correct market failures? In some situations, government failure arises because government intervention is unnecessary—that is, markets can adequately address their possible failures. Consequently, government intervention may prove to be counterproductive because market failure policies are flawed or poorly implemented and because policymakers, regardless of their intentions, are subject to political forces that enable certain interest groups to benefit at the expense of the public. In other situations, government action is called for but is again compromised by agency shortcomings and political forces.

---

1. In addition to the inefficiencies that they create, antitrust, economic regulation, and information policies entail considerable administrative and enforcement costs.

The fundamental underlying problem, as argued by Wolf (1979), is that the existence of government failure suggests the absence of an incentive to reconcile an intervention's costs and benefits to policymakers with its social costs and benefits. In contrast, it appears that in at least some instances market participants have greater incentives to correct market failures than the government has to correct these failures.

Market Robustness

Market failure is less common and less costly than might be expected because market forces tend to correct certain potential failures. Competition develops to prevent market power in input and output markets from being long-lived and often develops in markets that are believed to have "natural" entry barriers. As discussed later, the effects of economic deregulation suggest that experience is more instructive than theory about whether effective competition will develop in particular markets.

Market failure from imperfect information is limited because consumers are able to make informed choices by drawing on various publications, word-of-mouth, and their own experiences to learn about product quality and variety and rationally update their assessments of risk. For example, Mannering and Winston (1995) found that consumers' adoption of airbag-equipped automobiles during the 1990s was spurred by their friends' experiences with airbags and media reports about experiences that other motorists had with airbags. Calfee, Winston, and Stempski (2002) argued that the increasing demand for cholesterol-reducing drugs could be partly attributed to successful treatments that were being discussed among friends, coworkers, and physicians. The advent of the Internet has given consumers another way to become informed about the quality of products and services and to receive lower prices. Chevalier and Mayzlin (2003) pointed out that consumers pay attention to book reviews that are available at Amazon and Barnes and Noble. Web-based airline fares have made the lowest fares available to almost every traveler, and consumers who use the Internet to purchase a car have saved some $200 million a year because by learning about dealers' invoice prices and actual transactions prices, they have been more informed when they negotiate with car salespeople (Zettelmeyer, Scott Morton, and Silva-Risso 2001, 2005).

When not impeded by regulation, advertising can enable firms to overcome the inefficiencies created by the lack of property rights to most information. Among the positive externalities associated with advertising are better information about diet and health, opportunities to improve health through drug therapy, and the dangers of smoking (Calfee 1997).

Firms that produce faulty products or provide unsatisfactory services damage their reputations and incur financial costs. As pointed out by Jin, Kato, and List (2005), certification markets can provide information to reduce this possibility. For example, Underwriters Laboratories certifies the reliability of consumer and industrial products, Moody's and Standard and Poor's report bond ratings to inform investors about risk, and accounting companies audit financial reports for public corporations in an effort to deter and expose fraud. Firms have also instituted compensation policies to rectify cases when their product or service does not meet expectations. For example, when airlines oversell flights, they typically compensate travelers who voluntarily agree to be bumped more than they compensate travelers who are involuntarily bumped and are consequently subject to the U.S. Department of Transportation's compensation regulations.[2]

Finally, firms have strong incentives to maintain safe workplaces. Employers with workplaces that pose inherent risks to health benefit from self-selection in labor markets whereby workers who are most tolerant of risk are drawn to riskier jobs; higher wages must be paid to lure additional workers into these jobs. Without such heterogeneity, compensating wage premiums would probably be higher. But if a workplace is perceived as dangerous because workers have experienced a series of serious injuries, then the wage premium would have to rise considerably just to attract people who are tolerant of risky work. In general, firms also benefit from safe workplaces because production costs are lower, employees' productivity is higher, workers' compensation insurance premiums are reduced, and firms are more likely to avoid costly civil and possibly criminal litigation.

Market forces can even help lower the cost of some externalities. Households' choices of where to live and work reflect efficient sorting to reduce

2. See Keith L. Alexander, "Flying High By Getting Bumped," *Washington Post*, April 11, 2001. The industry policy evolved in response to a Civil Aeronautics Board rule that increased penalties for involuntary bumping. The volunteer auction system increased efficiency by delaying people who care least about waiting for the next departure and by enabling carriers to overbook at a higher rate and fly with fewer empty seats.

the costs of congestion, airplane noise, and air pollution. Calfee and Winston (1998) found that commuters with long commutes had lower values of travel time than commuters with shorter commutes, indicating that those commuters who dislike congestion the most reduce its cost by living closer to their workplaces. Morrison, Winston, and Watson (1999) argued that people who have a high tolerance for noise tend to live closer to a flight path and require less compensation, as reflected in lower housing prices, than people who have a low tolerance for noise. Banzhaf and Walsh (2005) reported evidence that whites tended to move out of areas with higher levels of air pollution and were replaced by (poorer) Hispanics. In addition, it has been estimated that black Americans are 79 percent more likely than whites to live in neighborhoods where industrial pollution is suspected of posing the greatest risks to health.[3] Although such sorting has raised concerns of "environmental" justice, it has lowered housing prices for the poor—a benefit that could dissipate if improvements in air quality cause wealthier people to move in and drive up rents for residents who do not own a home.[4]

Other market forces besides households' sorting help remedy externalities. Competition spurs firms to conduct R&D even if they cannot appropriate all of its benefits. Fish farms are a market response to declining fish stocks.[5] In addition, cooperation by some fishermen has helped to raise their catch in the past decade. For example, Acheson (1988) discussed how lobstermen adopted the practice of cutting a notch in the tail of a female lobster carrying masses of roe, so other lobstermen would know that these lobsters are breeding stock.

Some recent work even suggests that markets may exert forces that address multiple sources of potential failure. For example, Antweiler, Copeland, and Taylor (2001) found that freer trade enhanced product market competition and increased a nation's output, which called for cleaner production methods and helped improve the environment. Specifically, the authors found that sulfur dioxide fell by roughly the same

3. Associated Press, "More Blacks Live with Pollution," *New York Times*, December 13, 2005.

4. In contrast to residential sorting in response to air pollution, Greenstone and Gallagher (2005) did not find any evidence of residential sorting in response to hazardous wastes.

5. Some controversy currently exists over the extent to which fish farms disturb the natural environment for marine life.

amount in percentage terms that national income rose from more open international markets. Frankel and Rose (2005) reported a similar finding.

Government Agency Shortcomings

There is no question that many of the policy problems that government agencies face today are far more challenging than the problems they faced in an earlier era. In addition, as I discuss, policymakers' performance has improved in some areas. Nonetheless, it is fair to say that although government agencies may strive to solve social problems, they have frequently contributed to policy failures by their short-sightedness, inflexibility, and conflicts.

Some policies may have produced benefits when they were initially implemented or may be a well-intentioned response to an economic crisis, but policymakers have lacked the vision to modify or eliminate policies that are counterproductive in their current form. For example, agricultural price supports are essentially New Deal programs that were developed in the most tumultuous period in modern U.S. economic history. Current agriculture policy should reflect the economic realities of the times and eliminate these subsidies. Khan and Sokoloff (2001) suggested that the introduction of patent laws in the United States in the early nineteenth century spurred economic innovation and growth. However, a secular decline in patenting per capita began at the end of that century, even though the country continued to innovate and grow. It is possible that patents became less essential for fostering innovation as greater competition caused firms to increase their participation in this activity while individual inventors decreased their activity. The 1982 Federal Courts Improvement Act caused patent growth to resume, but the social gain generated by patent policy in today's economy is in doubt.

Antitrust offers another example of shortsighted policy. After taking several years to resolve a monopolization case, the Justice Department and the FTC often find that market conditions have changed, but they are unable to anticipate or account for new sources of competition that may eviscerate their reason for bringing a case. The antitrust authorities have found it difficult to formulate consent decrees in monopoly and merger cases that benefit consumers in the long run (Crandall and Winston 2003).

The failure of agencies to adjust their policies appropriately to generate socially desirable outcomes occurs in many situations. The Justice Department and the FTC have litigated price fixing and mergers that are not harmful to consumers (Crandall and Winston 2003); OSHA standards that are focused on capital equipment ignore the critical interactions between labor, equipment, and the workplace environment (Bartel and Thomas 1985); by allocating its funds in an inefficient manner, MSHA compromises any potential benefits from regulating coal mine safety (Kniesner and Leeth 2004); CPSC's priority rankings are at variance with benefit-cost ratios (Thomas 1988); the Transportation Department and the FDA have not anticipated consumers' offsetting behavior that has undermined their policies; and the EPA's command-and-control policies appear to pay insufficient attention to firms' costs and are based on implausibly high values of life (for example, Cropper and others 1992). Most agencies that address externalities either eschew prices as a mechanism for enhancing efficiency or, as in the case of fuel, cigarette, and alcohol taxes, set them inefficiently.

Still another source of inefficiency is agency policy that conflicts with either their own or another agency's basic objectives.[6] For example, the Securities and Exchange Commission is responsible for preventing companies from misleading the public about their financial condition. But the SEC has enacted entry regulations that have stifled competition among independent credit rating agencies that could provide investors with a valuable assessment of a company's creditworthiness because their access to a corporation's books is greater than the public's access (White 2002). Thus, regulation has reduced the effectiveness of a certification market by thwarting competition. The Transportation Department seeks to encourage fuel economy and promote safety, but the EPA's emissions regulations increase vehicle weight and reduce fuel economy and Transportation's CAFE standards increase the share of light trucks on the road, which reduces safety and fuel economy (Lave 1984; Godek 1997). The U.S. Forest Service is responsible for preserving public lands in their natural state, which means

---

6. As noted, the courts identified conditions that would uphold AT&T's claim of antitrust immunity because they were subject to FCC regulation, but in practice these conditions were not met.

that it should allow fires caused by lightning strikes to spread to some extent because they regenerate many tree species. However, the service has contained such fires, thereby allowing plant life that is able to reproduce without fires to overwhelm preexisting species (Nelson 2000). Recently, the Forest Service has permitted landscape-wide logging to reduce forest fires—a practice that is not believed by the scientific community to promote healthy forest growth. Finally, cooperative fishery management (known as conservation cartels) limits entry and lowers output but promotes conservation and ensures sustainable marine resources. However, these cartels have been found to violate antitrust laws (Adler 2005).

When viewed in their totality, market failure policies often conflict: policymakers want to use the antitrust laws to promote domestic competition, but they enact trade policies that are not justified on market failure grounds and disadvantage foreign firms that can compete with U.S. firms; policymakers try to lower the cost of transportation externalities, but they subsidize auto and urban transit; and so on. Generally, policymakers have made little effort to resolve intra- and interagency policy conflicts.

Political Forces

If it is easy—and it apparently is—to identify flaws in the design and implementation of market failure policies, why don't policymakers address these flaws and develop more efficient policies? George Stigler's answer is that the primary intent of government interventions is to redistribute income; thus, it would be unreasonable to expect that governmental favors obtained by competing interests would constitute social improvements.[7] Grossman and Helpman's (2005) answer is that a protectionist bias exists in majoritarian politics—in particular, they show that international trade policies favor specific factors of production.

One could argue that policymakers try to redistribute income as *efficiently as possible* (for example, see Becker 1983, 1985). But Winston and Maheshri (2006b) suggested that interest groups who receive rents "invest" in their stock of political capital to secure preferential treatment in the future. Thus, deadweight costs are not necessarily minimized subject to

---

7. Friedland (2002) synthesizes several of Stigler's papers that articulate this view.

political objectives. For example, farmers continue to support production quotas and price supports instead of a more efficient redistribution policy of lump-sum subsidies; all users of public transit pay fares below marginal cost instead of selected users being given vouchers; and truckers are subsidized for their use of the highways instead of paying an efficient pavement-wear tax and receiving lump-sum tax breaks based on vehicle miles traveled. And because the broad base of taxpayers tends to be less aware of or indifferent to specific welfare losses than well-organized interests are of their benefits (Olson 1965), imperfect information may also create an imbalance of political pressure that enables economically inefficient policies to persist.[8] It is therefore not surprising that well-defined interest groups, with the help of the government, are able to use their organizational and informational advantages to accrue economic rents inefficiently.

Table 6-2 summarizes illustrative studies identifying interest groups, such as selected firms and industries, farmers, unionized labor, social advocacy groups, urban and rural transportation interests, and general aviation, that influence market failure policies to promote their members' welfare. Congress is a powerful conduit for these interests through its appropriations to such agencies as the FTC and the Department of Justice and through its financing of public enterprises such as highways. Congress also passes legislation, such as bills containing agricultural subsidies and trade protection, which is influenced by and benefits narrow interests at the expense of consumer welfare. In fact, some of the direct beneficiaries are also members of Congress. During 1996–2000, agricultural subsidies were paid to farm operations that were owned in whole or in part by Senators Charles Grassley (Iowa), Richard Lugar (Indiana), Blanche Lincoln (Arkansas), and Sam Brownback (Kansas), and Representatives Marion Berry (Arkansas), Calvin Dooley (California), Charles Stenholm (Texas), Dennis Hastert (Illinois), and Bob Stump (Arizona).

---

8. Voters may not oppose the vast majority of redistribution that results from inefficient market failure policies as long as they get their particular subsidy. Consider Hartwell C. Herring's July 7, 2002, letter to the *New York Times Magazine*: "The Amtrak subsidy, which is minuscule compared to the bloated farm subsidy and pork-ridden defense budget, is one of the few direct benefits I get from the federal taxes I pay. I have a neighbor who is a dairy farmer. He probably collects more in subsidy from the government than he pays in taxes. Not me. I am one of the folks who pick up the tab, and I need my train service."

Table 6-2. *Interest Groups and Market Failure Policies*

Policy	Influential Interest Groups
Antitrust:	Congress can influence the activities of the Federal Trade Commission and the Justice Department through its appropriations for these agencies. There appears to be a bias in FTC case selection in favor of firms that operate in the jurisdiction of members of congressional committees that have important budgetary and oversight powers.[a]
Economic Regulation:	
Agricultural subsidies	Farmers and their lobbyists have been more successful in obtaining public assistance for certain commodities than for others. For example, producers of milk, sugar, peanuts, and wheat receive subsidies, but those producing cattle, eggs, hogs, and beef do not. The size of the producer group and whether the commodity is exported and/or subject to competition from imports influence whether support is given.[b]
Trade protection	Powerful unions seeking to protect the jobs of their members and industries facing foreign competition that are able to organize into an effective lobby have been highly influential in federal decisions to impose trade restrictions.[c]
Social Regulation:	
Occupational safety	The stringency of OSHA's interventions varies across industries and firms, reflecting the political power of these entities. Unionized and large firms incur much lower costs from occupational safety enforcement than smaller and nonunion firms.[d]
Consumption externalities	Antismoking and antidrinking advocacy groups successfully urge adoption of a "sin tax" on smoking and drinking. FAA noise regulations reflect the relative political power of homeowners and airlines rather than economic efficiency.[e]
Production externalities	Environmental and business advocacy groups influence the EPA to adopt industrial and water pollution policies that suit their interests. Regional interests influence and distort industrial pollution regulations. For example, the West and the South have opposed regulations that prevent significant deterioration of local air quality because such regulations limit their region's economic growth. The inefficiencies of hazardous waste programs reflect the political pressure to clean up less cost-effective sites dominated by white residents, rather than more cost-effective sites dominated by minority residents.[f]

(continued)

Table 6-2. *Interest Groups and Market Failure Policies* (continued)

Policy	Influential Interest Groups
Public Production:	
Highways	To maintain political support for a national highway system, numerous rural states with relatively low traffic volumes receive a disproportionately large share of highway funds, while states with high traffic volumes, such as California, receive a disproportionately smaller share of funds. Congressional members sitting on transportation committees secure higher project spending than other members secure. They also receive a larger share of funding that is appropriated for pork barrel demonstration projects that benefit their constituents. Lobbying organizations that represent motorists, such as the American Automobile Association, strongly oppose efforts to institute congestion pricing.[g]
Transit	The presence and level of urban transit subsidies are influenced by unionized labor, suppliers of transit capital, and patrons, especially upper-income suburban residents who use fixed rail. Subsidies are accrued by these interests in the form of above-market wages, excess profits for transit suppliers, and fares substantially below costs.[h]
Airports	Owners of corporate jets and small planes (general aviation) exert effective lobbying pressure on the FAA to maintain the current system of landing fees that charges them far less than the social cost of their use of runway capacity.[i]
Public Lands	Advocacy groups promoting the use of public lands for recreation or conservation oppose the adoption of user fees and exert pressure to keep user fees that are approved below marginal cost.[j]

a. Faith, Leavens, and Tollison (1982); Weingast and Moran (1983); Coate, Higgins, and McChesney (1995).

b. Gardner (1987).

c. Godek (1985); Kalt (1988).

d. Bartel and Thomas (1985).

e. Heien (1995); Morrison, Winston, and Watson (1999).

f. Portney (1990); Magat, Krupnick, and Harrington (1986); Pashigian (1985); Hamilton and Viscusi (1999).

g. Evans (1994); Johnson and Libecap (2000); Winston (2000); Knight (2005).

h. Winston and Shirley (1998).

i. Morrison (1987); Stiglitz (1998).

j. Gardner (1997).

Policy is also made by unelected bureaucrats who work at federal agencies and departments. McCubbins, Noll, and Weingast (1987) argued that the politics of these bureaucracies often mirror the same influences affecting Congress and the president. Thus, federal regulatory agencies such as OSHA, FAA, and EPA, and departments such as Transportation and Agriculture are also subject to interest group pressure that creates deadweight losses while often redistributing income from less affluent to more affluent citizens.

A few studies have tried to establish explicit links between the ways various interest groups compromise specific policies and the inefficiencies created. For example, Winston and Shirley (1998) found that certain socioeconomic groups (such as high-income residents) influenced urban rail transit fares and service, resulting in sharp deviations from efficient pricing and service guidelines. Knight (2004) analyzed congressional support for projects that were part of the 1998 Transportation Equity Act for the 21st Century, authorizing transportation spending for 1998–2003, and showed that representatives from politically powerful congressional districts supported highway demonstration projects to benefit their constituents. According to Knight, this support caused overall highway spending to increase and resulted in a deadweight loss of roughly ninety-six cents for every dollar spent on the projects, or more than $7 billion. Additional studies would help pin down the extent to which political forces contribute to government failure.

Looking to the future, the doubling of registered lobbyists in Washington between 2000 and 2005 (currently standing at roughly 35,000) indicates that elected and unelected policymakers are likely to be subject to even stronger political pressure from various interest groups. Indeed, the returns from lobbying have been large, with the relationship between clients' benefits and costs reported to approach 100:1 in some instances.[9] Greater competition among lobbyists may lower returns, but it may also increase the difficulty of designing and inducing the appropriate incentives to reduce government failure.

9. Jeffrey H. Birnbaum, "Clients' Rewards Keep K Street Lobbyists Thriving," *Washington Post*, February 14, 2006, p. A1.

7 | Market Failure and Social Goals Policies: Common Failures and Conflicts

Thus far, I have confined my assessment to policymakers' efforts to improve U.S. microeconomic efficiency by correcting market failures. However, American society, like any society, seeks to solve other social problems. U.S. policymakers have therefore enacted an array of social goals policies that can be categorized broadly as attempting to reduce poverty, ensure fairness in labor markets, and provide merit goods.[1]

Although these policies redistribute resources from one group of citizens for the benefit of another group of citizens, I do not believe that they conflict with efficiency to such an extent that policymakers and citizens must resign themselves to tolerating Okun's (1975) "leaky bucket"—that is, resource costs from redistributing income. My view is that social goals policies should be held to economic efficiency standards by determining whether they have accomplished their goals, and if so, whether they have

---

1. Policies to reduce poverty include direct financial assistance to poor families, interventions in the labor market to raise the earnings of the working poor, and specific (in-kind) benefits to disadvantaged individuals. Policies to promote fairness in labor markets include prohibitions on discrimination against potential employees on the basis of race, gender, or disability, and fair treatment in the workplace. Finally, the merit goods that American society believes every citizen is entitled to regardless of whether he or she can afford them include an education, the opportunity to own a home, insurance against certain events that could dramatically lower the quality of life (social insurance), and protection from criminals, hostile countries and terrorists, and natural disasters.

accomplished them at minimum cost to society. Accordingly, market failure and social goals policies should complement each other's objectives whenever possible instead of undermining them.

It is beyond the scope of this study to synthesize the voluminous empirical assessments of social goals policies. However, it is fair to suggest that a representative selection of the assessments draws conclusions that are broadly similar to assessments of market failure policies; namely, redistribution policies have often made little progress in achieving their goals while wasting considerable resources in the process.[2] Another important similarity is that social goals policies have been compromised by the same factors—unanticipated behavioral responses, poor program structure, and political forces—that have compromised market failure policies.

Disadvantaged and not-so-disadvantaged individuals have rationally responded to social goals policies in ways that have raised the policies' costs. Direct welfare assistance, food stamps, housing subsidies, Medicaid, and unemployment and disability insurance have encouraged recipients to reduce their search for employment. Notwithstanding its benefits, workers' compensation has induced workers to be less careful on the job and to file claims for non-work-related injuries (Meyer, Viscusi, and Durbin 1995). And firms have offset policies that have attempted to promote fair hiring and improve the terms of employment. Faced with potentially costly lawsuits for terminating female and disabled employees, firms have hired fewer of these workers (DeLeire 2000; Neumark and Stock 2001; Acemoglu and Angrist 2001). Forced to pay overtime wages and warn workers of impending plant closings, firms have reduced straight-time wages and found ways to close plants without providing advance notice (Trejo 1991; Addison and Blackburn 1994).

A few programs such as Head Start have made some progress toward their goals—for instance, to reduce the high school dropout rate (Garces, Thomas, and Currie 2002)—because they are streamlined and have appropriate goals that can be assessed. In many cases, however, multiple programs are used to accomplish the same goals. Thus, some programs overlap, such as Supplementary Security Income, Medicaid, and disability insurance to aid the elderly, and child care subsidies and the earned income

2. Some recent comprehensive assessments include Moffitt (2003) on policies to reduce poverty, Ellwood (2001) on labor market interventions, Borjas (1999) on immigration policy, and Feldstein (2005) on social insurance policies.

tax credit to assist low-income households with children. Other programs and policies conflict, such as job training programs that seek to enhance employability while in-kind benefits discourage some recipients from seeking a job, or immigration policy that has recently allowed the share of households in poverty to expand while welfare policy attempts to help households escape poverty.

Finally, social goals policies are clearly subject to political pressures, as vividly exemplified by the lobbying prowess of the AARP (formerly American Association of Retired Persons), which has helped to ensure that nearly 40 percent of the federal budget is for the benefit largely of the elderly (that is, Social Security, Medicare, and other programs). Congress has historically revised the minimum wage in accordance with the relative political strength of unions and firms (Sobel 1999). Firms and agricultural interests that rely on low-wage Mexican labor pressure Congress to adopt an immigration policy that increases their access to these workers (Reynolds and McCleery 1988). And, of course, the so-called Iron Triangle—military contractors, their allies in the Pentagon, and allies in Congress—is a powerful force for maintaining support for antiquated or unneeded new weapons and flawed projects. Indeed, military contractors spend more than $50 million a year lobbying Congress.[3]

In theory, market failure and social goals policies should complement each other. By enhancing market efficiency and not creating rents that adversely redistribute income, market failure policies should make resources available that could be used for social goals. By redistributing income in an efficient manner, social goals policies should not significantly reduce market efficiency. Given their common problems and the sources of these problems, however, it is not surprising that in practice social goals and market failure policies have conflicted.

Social goals policies have exacerbated market failure by distorting the workings of or impeding improvements in potentially efficient markets. For example, Congress established the E-rate program in 1996 that offered substantial subsidies to public schools and libraries to buy telecommunications services like wiring classrooms and connecting to the Internet. Congress should have considered the most efficient way to finance the subsidy such

---

3. Leslie Wayne, "So Much for the Plan to Scrap Old Weapons," *New York Times*, December 22, 2002, p. 1.

as a lump-sum tax. Or if public schools were run more efficiently, they may have had sufficient resources to support Internet service. In any case, the subsidies were funded by higher taxes on interstate telephone service, which distorts the workings of an efficient market. Hausman (1998) estimated that the cost of the E-rate program was $2.25 billion a year (not all of which was used for Internet wiring), while the additional cost to raise the requisite funds through taxation was $2.36 billion a year because taxes were imposed on price-elastic services. Thus, an ill-conceived approach to achieve a social goal created a large excess burden that could have been avoided if the goal were accomplished in a more efficient manner.

Policies to improve the efficiency of urban transit, such as abandoning lightly used routes and raising fares to reduce operating deficits, are often opposed because transit operations are (erroneously) claimed to provide an indispensable service to the poor (Winston 2000). Thus, the efficiency of public production is compromised because it is enlisted to address a social goal that should be addressed by policies that seek to reduce poverty. If policymakers are committed to using urban transit policy for that purpose, the most efficient way to do so would be to enhance the mobility of low-income users with vouchers, for example, without distorting transit prices and service.

I have discussed how efficient pricing of externalities such as automobile congestion and pollution could reduce the wasteful expenditures associated with current policies while reducing externality costs and improving social welfare. Some policymakers, however, have opposed using prices to address automobile externalities on the grounds that they are likely to harm low-income motorists. Thus, efficient reforms of market failure policies are impeded because they appear to conflict with social goals. But the conflict is exaggerated because efficient externality policies would make more resources available for redistribution that may contribute to a more effective welfare policy. For example, some of the revenues generated by efficient congestion tolls could be used to fund transportation vouchers for low-income travelers.

Policymakers create doubt about their commitment to social goals when they fail to reform inefficient market failure policies that adversely affect income distribution. For example, by raising the price of basic foodstuffs, milk products, and clothing, agricultural and trade regulations make life more difficult for poor households and are at variance with policies to reduce poverty. Another example is Superfund resources that are disproportionately spent on affluent rather than poorer neighborhoods (Hamilton and Viscusi 1999). If these resources were used more efficiently by cleaning up sites in order of the lowest cost per case of cancer prevented to the highest cost, minority neighborhoods would be cleaned up first. Still another example is environmental regulatory enforcement that pays much less attention to the polluting activities of plants located in poor neighborhoods than to the activities of plants located in higher-income neighborhoods (Gray and Shadbegian 2004; Bandyopadhyay and Horowitz 2006). Finally, public production of such services as urban rail transit, highways, intercity rail, and the like undoubtedly benefits higher-income households more than it benefits lower-income households. However, the inefficient financing and operation of these services have produced large deficits that must be covered by additional taxes that disproportionately add to the economic woes of the working poor.

The aftermath of Hurricane Katrina provides researchers with an opportunity to identify how an ineffective combination of policies designed to correct market failure and pursue social goals contributed to the catastrophe. For example, how efficient were public financing and management of water projects in the Gulf Coast region? Could the massive flooding have been prevented by efficient investment? Did the failure to prevent the flooding harm poor residents of the affected areas more than it harmed wealthy residents, in part because public housing and public assistance may have concentrated poor residents in areas below sea level? Are public assistance to victims of Katrina and public investment to rehabilitate New Orleans being conducted fairly and efficiently? Unfortunately, the answers to these questions are likely to provide additional examples of how market failure and social goals policies have failed to complement each other.

8 | *Policy Recommendations Motivated by Policymakers' Learning*

The ultimate purpose of this assessment is to identify ways that market failure policies can be improved. But unless policymakers have shown that they are capable of improving these policies, it is naïve to believe that any policy recommendations will have a constructive effect. My static assessment has identified few policy successes, but, in fact, policymakers have learned from counterproductive policies in certain areas and appropriately reformed their policies to varying degrees. I draw on these improvements to suggest other plausible ways in which policymakers could enhance the efficiency of market failure policies.

Learning

It is as difficult to offer a definitive explanation of why policymakers correct deficiencies in some of their policies as it is to explain why they institute inefficient policies in the first place. In any case, it appears that policymakers' actions toward all areas of possible market failure have benefited from basic insights from economics research about those policies that clearly do not work and alternative policies that may be successful.

Antitrust

Stigler (1982) argued that economists greeted the 1890 Sherman Antitrust Act with coolness if not downright hostility, but that support for antitrust policy steadily grew in the 1950s and 1960s. Today, I would say that economists still have a favorable view of antitrust, but they are much less supportive of an "activist" antitrust policy than they once were.

Antitrust policy has evolved by incorporating and benefiting from professional understanding of market competition and firm behavior. For example, Peltzman (2005) synthesized Aaron Director's (mainly oral) scholarly contributions that have influenced antitrust authorities to shift the emphasis from monopoly to efficiency as the primary motive for business practices like tie-in selling and resale price maintenance and to be skeptical of allegations of predatory pricing, thus reducing the number of cases brought in response to these actual or alleged practices. In addition, antitrust authorities have been more receptive to efficiency arguments in support of (particularly vertical) mergers and less likely to establish and enforce an arbitrary limit to industry concentration.[1] As I have argued, it is doubtful that the antitrust authorities have brought many cases that have enhanced consumer welfare. At the same time, they are probably less likely today to be prosecuting and possibly discouraging efficient firm behavior.

Economic Regulation

Policymakers' efforts to reform certain existing economic regulations, withdraw others, and refrain from instituting significant new regulations reflect considerable learning in this area of policy.

Agricultural and trade regulation have seen some positive reforms. For example, the 1996 Federal Agriculture Improvement and Reform Act reduced price supports for peanuts and allowed quota rights for domestic consumption to become transferable within a state, enabling lower-cost farms to displace higher-cost farms (Friedman 1999). In addition, Gardner (2002) pointed out that the 2002 farm bill—the Farm Security and Rural Investment Act—reduced distortions to production decisions by making

1. In 1969 the Neal Commission recommended that the four-firm concentration ratio in most industries should be limited to 70 percent.

lump-sum payments to landowners. As noted, multilateral agreements have gradually reduced trade restrictions. Agriculture and trade regulations still incur sizable efficiency costs, but policymakers appear capable of making efficient reforms and may conceivably fulfill the hope expressed periodically by recent presidential administrations of ending counterproductive government intervention in these areas.

The federal government has relaxed price, entry, and exit regulations to varying degrees in telephony and cable television, resulting in lower long-distance rates (Crandall and Hausman 2000) and more viewing options (Crandall and Furchtgott-Roth 1996). Vogelsang (2002) described how government has improved remaining price regulation, primarily in telecommunications, by replacing rate-of-return regulation with so-called incentive regulation. In practice, regulatory reform amounts to price caps that provide an incentive for cost reductions and price rebalancing.

The federal government achieved a major policy success when it largely deregulated the pricing, entry, and exit decisions of firms in the banking, brokerage, intercity transportation, and natural gas industries. Beginning in the late 1970s, economic deregulation spurred competition among incumbent firms and new entrants in each industry. The intensified competitive environment and operating freedom caused firms to lower costs and to become more innovative, thereby reducing prices and improving service quality. Consumer benefits have amounted to hundreds of billions of dollars (Winston 1998).

Finally, policymakers have been less inclined to impose significant new economic regulations to influence behavior. For example, by the late 1970s, prices of most fossil fuels were subjected to inefficient federal government control (that is, price ceilings) in response to the rise in crude oil prices. (Prices were decontrolled in 1981.) Today, the federal government would be highly unlikely to impose price ceilings on fossil fuels, despite recent real price increases in crude oil comparable to those during the 1970s.[2]

---

2. Unfortunately, the state of Hawaii put a price cap on gasoline prices in response to higher fuel prices in the summer of 2005. Research by Jack Suyderhoud of the University of Hawaii found that since the caps started, gasoline prices in Hawaii actually increased compared with prices on the mainland that were not subject to price caps. Apparently, the caps facilitated tacit collusion by dealers who set prices as high as the gas cap formula allowed. After an eight-month experiment, Hawaii gave up on price caps.

Social Regulations

The cost of social regulations remains excessive, but policymakers have reformed a few regulations and introduced new policies that have the potential to enhance social welfare. The FTC has gradually adopted the view that advertising is an essential part of the competitive process that provides information that may benefit consumers. Thus the FTC has recently—and appropriately—taken a relatively lax approach to information policy in this area. In 1997 the FDA allowed drug companies to provide direct-to-consumer advertising on electronic media. Consumers benefited from the information about new drug treatments, but they engaged in offsetting behavior by using the treatments (such as tobacco cessation products) so that they could maintain somewhat less-healthy lifestyles (Iizuka and Jin 2005). As noted, the FDA's introduction of user fees to expedite drug evaluations has helped improve the flow of new drugs on the market. Other information policies that may have produced benefits include hazardous warning labels and the EPA's Toxic Release Inventory Program.

Policymakers have also been more receptive to using market-oriented policies such as emissions trading to address externalities. Such policies have lowered the costs of reducing pollution and if applied more widely have the potential to generate substantial savings.

I have identified several drawbacks of patent policy, including the 1982 Federal Courts Improvement Act, which may have increased the costs of the system. But beneficial reforms are possible, as evidenced by the 1984 Hatch-Waxman Act that changed patent terms in the pharmaceutical drug industry while stimulating competition that reduced consumer prices.

Public Production

Public production tries to correct market failures primarily by disbursing revenue rather than by attempting to influence consumer or firm behavior. By failing to set efficient prices that reflect the costs of using the nation's infrastructure and certain services, government policy has produced substantial inefficiencies and large deficits. Recently, a few cities have experimented with a variant of congestion pricing by instituting high-occupancy toll (HOT) lanes, which enable motorists to pay a toll to use a less congested lane(s) normally reserved for carpools. The experiments indicate that policymakers may finally be willing to use the price mechanism to some degree to allocate scarce highway capacity. Broader adoption of road pricing may be encouraged by funding for fifteen variable-pricing programs contained in the federal transportation bill passed in 2005.

In sum, policymakers have shown that they have the capacity to learn from and improve deficient policies.[3] They have slowly accepted the view that consumers and firms contribute to market efficiency by pursuing their own interests and that it is difficult to use regulations to "command and control" these agents to correct market failures efficiently. In addition, policymakers have recently shown some willingness to introduce policies that could improve the efficiency of public infrastructure and services. To be sure, market failure policies still continue to impose large efficiency costs on the U.S. economy. But enlightened—and cautiously encouraged—by the evolution of policymakers' behavior, I offer constructive policy recommendations that may eventually receive serious consideration.

Policy Recommendations

The market failures that the federal government has tried to correct have become increasingly more challenging. For example, to the extent that public sector involvement was necessary to provide a socially beneficial service that the private sector could not offer, federal highway policy in the 1950s and 1960s simply had to disburse grants to help build a network of interstate highways. Today, the federal government continues to disburse money for highways, but it must also confront numerous problems such as rising congestion, a physically deteriorating road system, and adapting and paying for new technology that promises to increase travel speeds and safety.

Given that government has consistently failed to correct market failures, it is unlikely to start being more successful now, particularly when it is facing more difficult problems. While policymakers have shown some capacity to learn, little evidence exists that market failure policies have significantly improved because government has regulated better or spent

3. It is conceivable that policymakers would learn more about the (in)effectiveness of their policies if federal actions were routinely monitored retrospectively for their economic performance. But the U.S. Government Accountability Office (2005) has concluded that this rarely happens.

money more wisely. Perhaps if all the federal agencies that contribute to the formation and implementation of market failure policies had the autonomy of the Federal Reserve and the leadership of someone like Alan Greenspan, they might successfully reform their policies. Unfortunately, the Federal Reserve's recent performance is unique.

How can policy be improved? My first recommendation is that policymakers should pause and truly absorb the fact that government generally cannot be counted on to correct market failures efficiently by itself. Second, it is important for policymakers to acknowledge that the few microeconomic policies that have improved efficiency—which the federal government eventually grew to support—stem from market-oriented approaches. Moreover, evidence is increasingly suggesting that this approach can be applied to various policy areas. In other cases, our knowledge is insufficient to offer strong policy recommendations.

The absence of hard evidence that antitrust policy has produced sizable consumer benefits should concern policymakers. At the same time, the gaps in our knowledge about the effects of antitrust policy, especially how it deters anticompetitive behavior, suggest that it is premature to suggest major reforms. As indicated by Crandall and Winston (2003), until additional scholarly evidence becomes available, the Federal Trade Commission and the Department of Justice should focus on the most significant and egregious violations, such as blatant price fixing and merger-to-monopoly, and treat most other apparent threats to competition with benign neglect.

The ability of markets to accomplish what government policy could not was clearly revealed when the federal government initiated economic deregulation. Deregulation revealed that economic regulation, as enforced by various regulatory agencies, was counterproductive because it was creating more problems than it was solving—and imposing higher costs over time. For example, regulation prevented railroads from reducing their costs by abandoning excess track and from attracting more freight by negotiating price and service packages with shippers; thus, the industry was losing traffic to trucks, earning low rates of return, and in danger of becoming nationalized. When railroads were deregulated, carriers abandoned unprofitable routes, improved the efficiency of their operations (often through mergers), gave shippers an incentive to reduce their rates by shipping large traffic volumes at lower cost, provided faster and more reliable service, and reversed the long-term decline in traffic. Indeed, some economists were surprised that by preventing market forces from evolving, regulation had harmed both railroads *and* shippers (Winston 1993).

Generally, deregulation's success illustrated that many markets are sufficiently robust to prevent failures that may be caused by entry barriers, such as scale economies, and that such barriers may actually be created by regulatory restrictions on firms' operations.[4]

Deregulation could generate additional consumer benefits in communications, while electricity deregulation could in the long run lead to substantial gains to commercial and residential users by encouraging innovations in renewable resources, real-time pricing, and the like. These potential welfare improvements, however, have been indefinitely postponed by agency and governmental mismanagement and political wrangling that have delayed constructive regulatory reform. Contrary to popular impressions, communication and electricity services have been more prone to government failure than to market failure, but it may take decades before policymakers institute an effective deregulation strategy.[5]

Policymakers should also heed economists' long-standing calls to eliminate regulations in agriculture and international trade. Some small positive steps have been taken in that direction, but it would be desirable if future actions were much more comprehensive and permanent.

Turning to social regulations, information policies have generally not been found to produce much benefit for consumers. The costs of FDA drug evaluations were reduced by adopting user fees to expedite the evaluations. As in

4. For example, railroads were originally regulated because it was believed that they exhibited large scale economies that would lead to destructive competition in an unregulated market. Deregulation enabled railroads to shed excess capacity that had been created by regulatory restrictions on abandoning track and prohibitions on negotiating contract rates. Under contract rates, shippers would receive a lower rate by agreeing to ship a certain volume of freight and by providing return shipments at the destination, thus reducing the percentage of railcars with an empty backhaul.

5. Cable television was reregulated in 1992 with mandated price reductions of at least 10 percent, but Crawford (2000) found that reregulation led to no change in consumer welfare. Crandall and Hausman (2000) and Crandall (2005a) discussed how the 1996 Telecommunications Act has frustrated the development of local telephone and cable competition. Indeed, local telephony regulation still generates deadweight losses. California's attempt to deregulate electricity was a well-publicized disaster, but as pointed out by McFadden (2001), the experience was another episode in a long cycle of mismanaged regulation and partial deregulation. The source of the recent crisis was rigid regulation of retail prices in the face of rapid increases in wholesale prices driven by rising fuel prices and growing demand in the national market. A detailed discussion of the California experience is given in Joskow (2001), and various issues surrounding regulatory reform of electricity are analyzed in Griffin and Puller (2005).

the case of antitrust, the ability of certain policies such as FDA drug evalua-tions to deter harmful products needs to be quantified before additional pol-icy recommendations can be offered. Sulfur dioxide emissions trading pro-grams are another example of how government policy has produced benefits by designing a framework in which market forces could address a market fail-ure. The application of trading programs should be extended to reduce water pollution, automobile emissions, and other sources of air pollution in a more cost-effective manner than the current command-and-control policies allow. It may even be possible to allow private companies to compete to clean up hazardous wastes, with jobs based on the most cost-effective bids instead of the EPA's decisions on how to disburse Superfund monies. Finally, most technology policies have not been found to yield high returns and do not merit continued support. An exception, not surprisingly, is that society is likely to benefit from increased support for academic research. Further evi-dence is needed about the welfare properties of the patent system before major policy reforms can be suggested.

The vast inefficiencies of public infrastructure and other public services suggest that greater reliance on market forces may improve performance.[6] Research has begun to explore the benefits from privatizing highways, bus and rail transit, intercity rail, airports, and postal services and from allow-ing private enterprises to manage inland waterway projects, public lands, and federal research institutions.[7] Winston and Shirley (1998), for exam-ple, provide preliminary evidence that privatizing public transit would lower urban bus and rail operating costs, improve productivity, and elimi-nate public subsidies (although fares would probably rise). Given urban rail's questionable social desirability, some form of privatization would appear to merit serious consideration. Indeed, several countries have exper-imented with privatizing their transportation services with some encour-aging results (Gomez-Ibanez and Meyer 1993). Geddes (2005) pointed out that by privatizing their postal service, countries such as Germany have

6. Auctions represent a market approach that has been used to give private firms access to quasi-public goods such as airwaves emanating from the electromagnetic spectrum and the oil and gas reserves of the outer continental shelf. The federal government recently conducted an auction to allow companies to use the airwaves for wireless communications but unfortunately decided to give broad-casters a part of the spectrum for HDTV instead of selling it.

7. The transportation legislation passed in 2005 gives states the option to attract private invest-ments in roads, which at least opens the possibility for greater private sector participation in infra-structure provision.

generated benefits in lower costs and better service. Geddes (2003) outlined an approach to eliminate the U.S. postal service monopoly and allow competition in letter delivery that would lower first-class rates and improve service.

To summarize, in those cases where it has been possible to fully assess the effectiveness of government policy to correct a market failure, it appears that such failures could be remedied more efficiently by crafting policies that incorporate market-oriented incentives. Of course, it is possible to raise doubts about whether policymakers have sufficient incentives to initiate such major changes in policy. Becker (1983) and Friedman (1999) suggested that efficient reforms may occur only because a deal can be reached that makes everyone better off (or at least leaves some people no worse off). Winston and Maheshri (2006b) argued that inefficient policies are rarely reformed, but they acknowledged that efficient reforms may occur if the inefficiencies become too large.

Market forces have also limited market failure in the presence of market power, imperfect information, and externalities from innovation. Some aspects of government policy may also be reducing market failure (such as deterring unlawful competitive behavior and harmful products), but as noted such benefits have yet to be quantified. Additional research is therefore necessary before we can identify the socially desirable mix of government intervention, if any, and market incentives to address these problems.

9 | *Microeconomics Policy Research and the Policy Community*

Economists who conduct theoretical or empirical studies of policy issues undoubtedly wish to have an impact beyond the academic community. Microeconomics policy research can contribute and has contributed to policy formation by attracting the attention of government staff members who are trained in economics and can distill the essential ideas for policymakers. For instance, according to Derthick and Quirk (1985), economic deregulation would never have occurred if microeconomists had not generally supported it through their research. DOJ's and FTC's approach to antitrust policy and FTC's approach to information policy have benefited from economists' greater understanding of market behavior. Notwithstanding these contributions and others, I believe that the academic community could have a greater and more constructive impact on policy by making a concerted effort to close important gaps in our theoretical and empirical research into market failures and by integrating new findings with the broad themes of why market failure policies have been deficient and how they can improve.

Theory

Following the development and refinement of the Arrow-Debreu model of a perfectly competitive economy in the 1950s and 1960s, the bulk of microeconomic theory has devoted far more attention to identifying and characterizing potential sources of market failure than to recognizing and analyzing the causes of government failure.[1] Posner (1993) interpreted the "interventionist" concepts that have been developed as invitations for government action. Given the evidence presented here, it would be desirable to build on the limited research available to have a better theoretical understanding of the sources of government failure. For example, why does the government seem unable to resolve intra- and interagency policy conflicts? Why do policymakers eschew efficient pricing for command-and-control policies (Buchanan and Tullock 1975)? Under what economic and political conditions are policymakers likely to replace inefficient policies with more efficient market-oriented reforms (Noll 1989a, 1989b; Peltzman 1989)?

Given that markets appear to be more robust to failures (that is, self-correcting) than recent developments in microeconomic theory have suggested, it would be useful to reconsider the conditions under which market-oriented solutions to current government failures are likely to be effective.[2] Theoretical analyses should also be cautious about recommending policies that presume the existence of market failure, such as strategic trade policy that seeks to capture the available rents in imperfectly competitive international markets. Harris (1994) indicates the gains from this policy are small.

Recent theoretical work in behavioral economics and social norms also indicates significant potential for market failure because consumers do not always behave rationally in various market and social settings. It is, of course, premature to assess the substantive content of these lines of research. But to contribute to public policy, behavioral economists will have to quantify the importance of the alleged concerns about market performance and produce evidence that the government could formulate and implement policies that would improve matters.

1. The field of public choice is concerned with government failure, but I would suggest that this literature is not given much attention in most microeconomic theory texts or courses.
2. Theoretical developments have identified the potential for a market failure to exist, but in practice the failure has been addressed to a large degree by market forces. Such developments include game theoretic derivations of anticompetitive strategies, demonstrations that network externalities could be a source of market power, and models of asymmetric and imperfect information.

Empirics

Although economists have assessed a remarkable range of market failure policies, we have only a very rough idea of the costs and benefits of some of them. As noted, I did not offer strong policy recommendations to improve antitrust and information policy because sufficient evidence regarding their potentially important deterrence effects was not available. In addition, further research is needed to assess the welfare properties of the patent system. Empirical research can help justify and guide privatization experiments to improve on financing of public enterprises. Of course, policymakers may not be immediately receptive to privatization proposals. Nonetheless, it is important for researchers to explore the matter because a crisis, such as intolerable budget deficits, may arise that causes policymakers to consider privatization as a viable policy option.[3]

Policy debates that could lead to beneficial policy reform often do not move beyond square one because they fail to acknowledge the existence of an accumulated body of empirical evidence that significantly advances our understanding of the problem—either directly or indirectly by shedding light on a similar debate. Thus, it is important for empirical researchers to build on and accentuate the broad themes that have emerged from the evidence to date on the effects of market failure policies. It may not be obvious to policymakers that policies to promote automobile safety and policies to promote conservation of fish stocks are compromised for similar reasons (offsetting behavior), or that market forces strongly limit the exercise of market power as well as encourage energy conservation. Policymakers are likely to be more responsive to arguments that apply to a wide range of experiences with government intervention than to arguments that appear to apply to a seemingly isolated case.

---

3. Feldstein (2005) recounts an experience that illustrates the importance of scholars developing research in advance of policymakers' interest. According to Feldstein, President Reagan was unhappy with the state of Social Security and wondered whether an investment-based system based on personal retirement accounts could replace a pay-as-you-go system. In his capacity as chairman of Reagan's Council of Economic Advisors, Feldstein was not aware of a feasible transition that would not place an excessive burden on the transition generation. Feldstein now argues that subsequent research does offer a feasible transition plan, but he regrets that a solution was not available when Reagan was interested in one.

A Final Plea

It is, of course, common for an economist to suggest issues that other economists should work on, especially when the work involves issues that he or she cares about. At the same time, I cannot ignore observations made by economics journal editors such as Borts (1981) that economists are "notoriously reluctant to invest time in writing serious policy papers that will be submitted for refereeing and subject to outright rejection." Ellison (2002) has argued that social norms within the economics profession increasingly emphasize technical craftsmanship and polish; thus, policy papers, which often do not exhibit these features, may face even greater obstacles to acceptance. He also suggested that policy papers that do eventually get published are taking much longer to get into print, making them less relevant for live debates. The current professional incentives and obstacles appear to shed light on Stigler's (1982) observation that active public policy carries no assurance that fundamental economic research relevant to that policy area will flourish.

That said, the issues that I speak of are of vital interest to the profession and to the world not only because they constitute an important part of government activity, but also because broad evidence exists that inefficient microeconomic policies can be a significant constraint on a country's growth and development. For example, cross-country studies by Alesina and others (2003) and Djankov and others (2000) find that tight regulations of product market competition stymie investment and are associated with a relatively greater size of the unofficial economy. Barro (1998) documented that microeconomic policies that fail to enrich human capital, improve market efficiency, and spur innovation have negative effects on growth rates. The concerns with government failure that I have raised here are also relevant for the emerging field of comparative political economy, which is exploring influences on policy choices and consequent economic outcomes.

Underlying the aggregate findings of cross-country studies are hundreds of small—and not so small—deadweight losses that need to be measured and understood to identify common themes that can provide constructive guidance for improving microeconomic policies in the United States and abroad. The scope and magnitude of this research effort obviously requires careful empirical work, including original data collection and deep institutional knowledge. From experience, I know it is easy to study competition policy in the U.S. airline industry, where data are readily available and the institutions are widely known, but it is another matter to understand the details of water regulations and obtain accurate measurements of contaminates.

In short, the economics profession should encourage a broader range as well as different styles of research by giving more respect to high-quality policy studies on specific and perhaps small issues that accumulate in importance. Financial incentives provided by the policy community would also be helpful. The following proposals are suggestive but by no means exhaustive:

—Teaching-oriented colleges that require some degree of scholarly engagement could offer a policy-oriented path to tenure in economics, where recognized expertise in economic analysis of certain policy problems would be key.

—Government agencies and foundations such as the National Science Foundation could be encouraged to expand their funding for policy-related work. For example, the Robert Wood Johnson Foundation has helped promote the research programs of health economists.

—Ph.D.-granting institutions could encourage one of the three essays that often make up a doctoral dissertation to contain institution-intensive, policy-relevant material.

—Finally, the American Economic Association has recently announced that it intends to publish new field journals. Hopefully, some space will be devoted to well-done policy articles, even if they lack new theoretical or empirical innovations. Accordingly, other journals might follow the association's lead.

For now, I conclude that scholarly research has consistently found substantial failure in government's efforts to correct market failures and that neither failure is often corrected in an appropriate manner. But the situation is not insolvable because policymakers have shown some capacity to learn. The common problem with market failure policies has suggested a common solution calling for policies that rely on a market-oriented framework. I sincerely hope the economics profession and the policy community will build on the scholarship that underlies these conclusions with the ambitious aim of opening the door to greater wisdom.

References

Acemoglu, Daron, and Joshua D. Angrist. 2001. "Consequences of Employment Protection? The Case of the Americans with Disabilities Act." *Journal of Political Economy* 109 (October): 915–57.

Acheson, James M. 1988. *The Lobster Gangs of Maine.* Hanover, N.H.: University Press of New England.

Addison, John T., and McKinley L. Blackburn. 1994. "Has WARN Warned? The Impact of Advance-Notice Legislation on the Receipt of Advance Notice." *Journal of Labor Research* 15 (Winter): 83–90.

Adie, Douglas K. 1989. *Monopoly Mail: Privatizing the U.S. Postal Service.* Brunswick, N.J.: Transaction Publishers.

Adler, Jonathan H. 2005. "Conservation Cartels." *Regulation* 27 (Winter): 38–45.

Akerlof, George. 1970. "The Market for Lemons: Quality Uncertainty and the Market Mechanism." *Quarterly Journal of Economics* 85 (August): 488–500.

Alesina, Alberto, Silvia Ardagna, Giuseppe Nicoletti, and Fabio Schiantarelli. 2003. "Regulation and Investment." Working Paper 9560. Cambridge, Mass.: National Bureau of Economic Research (March).

Androkovich, R. A., and K. R. Stollery. 1989. "Regulation of Stochastic Fisheries: A Comparison of Alternative Methods in the Pacific Halibut Industry." *Marine Resource Economics* 6: 109–22.

Antweiler, Werner, Brian R. Copeland, and M. Scott Taylor. 2001. "Is Free Trade Good for the Environment?" *American Economic Review* 91(September): 877–908.

Baker, Jonathan. 2003. "The Case for Antitrust Enforcement." *Journal of Economic Perspectives* 17 (Fall): 27–50.

Bandyopadhyay, Sushenjit, and John Horowitz. 2006. "Do Plants Overcomply with Water Pollution Regulations? The Role of Discharge Variability." *Topics in Economic Analysis and Policy* 6.

Banzhaf, H. Spencer, and Randall P. Walsh. 2005. "Do People Vote With Their Feet?: An Empirical Test of Environmental Gentrification." Working paper. Washington: Resources for the Future (July).

Barro, Robert. 1998. *Determinants of Economic Growth: A Cross-Country Empirical Study.* MIT Press.

Bartel, Ann P., and Lacy Glenn Thomas. 1985. "Direct and Indirect Effects of Regulation: A New Look at OSHA's Impact." *Journal of Law and Economics* 28 (April): 1–25.

Bator, Francis M. 1958. "The Anatomy of Market Failure." *Quarterly Journal of Economics* 72 (August): 351–79.

Becker, Gary S. 1983. "A Theory of Competition among Pressure Groups for Political Influence." *Quarterly Journal of Economics* 98 (August): 371–400.

———. 1985. "Public Policies, Pressure Groups, and Deadweight Costs." *Journal of Public Economics* 28: 329–47.

Benham, Lee. 1972. "The Effect of Advertising on the Price of Eyeglasses." *Journal of Law and Economics* 15 (October): 337–52.

Block, Michael Kent, Frederick Carl Nold, and Joseph Gregory Sidak. 1981. "The Deterrent Effect of Antitrust Enforcement." *Journal of Political Economy* 89 (June): 429–45.

Blomquist, Glen C. 1988. *The Regulation of Motor Vehicle and Traffic Safety.* Boston: Kluwer Academic Publishers.

Boal, William M., and Michael R. Ransom. 1997. "Monopsony in the Labor Market." *Journal of Economic Literature* 35 (March): 86–112.

Booth, Alison L. 1995. *The Economics of the Trade Union.* Cambridge University Press.

Borjas, George J. 1999. *Heaven's Door: Immigration Policy and the American Economy.* Princeton University Press.

Borts, George. 1981. "Report of the Managing Editor." *American Economic Review* 71 (May): 452–64.

Brueckner, Jan K. 2002. "Airport Congestion When Carriers Have Market Power." *American Economic Review* 92 (December): 1357–75.

Buchanan, James, and Gordon Tullock. 1975. "Polluters' Profits and Political Responses: Direct Controls Versus Taxes." *American Economic Review* 65 (March): 139–47.

Burton, David A. 1996. "Software Developers Want Changes in Patent and Copyright Law." *Michigan Telecommunications and Technology Law Review* 2: 87-91.

Burtraw, Dallas, Ranjit Bharvirkar, and Meghan McGuiness. 2003. "Uncertainty and the Net Benefits of NO_x Emissions Reductions from Electricity Generation." *Land Economics* 79 (August): 382–401.

Burtraw, Dallas, and Karen Palmer. 2004. "SO$_2$ Cap-and-Trade Program in the United States: A 'Living Legend' of Market Effectiveness." In *Choosing Environmental Policy: Comparing Instruments and Outcomes in the United States and Europe*, edited by Winston Harrington, Richard D. Morgenstern, and Thomas Sterner. Washington: Resources for the Future.

Cady, John F. 1976. "An Estimate of the Price Effects of Restrictions on Drug Price Advertising." *Economic Inquiry* 14 (December): 493–510.

Calfee, John E. 1997. *Fear of Persuasion: A New Perspective on Advertising and Regulation*. London: Agora.

Calfee, John E., and Debra Jones Ringold. 1994. "The 70% Majority: Enduring Consumer Beliefs About Advertising." *Journal of Public Policy and Marketing* 13 (Fall): 228–38.

Calfee, John, and Clifford Winston. 1998. "The Value of Automobile Travel Time: Implications for Congestion Policy." *Journal of Public Economics* 69 (July): 83–102.

Calfee, John E., Clifford Winston, and Randolph Stempski. 2002. "Direct-To-Consumer Advertising and the Demand for Cholesterol Reducing Drugs." *Journal of Law and Economics* 45 (October, part II): 673–90.

Carlson, Curtis, Dallas Burtraw, Maureen Cropper, and Karen Palmer. 2000. "Sulfur Dioxide Control by Electric Utilities: What Are the Gains from Trade?" *Journal of Political Economy* 108 (December): 1293–1326.

Carlton, Dennis W., Gustavo E. Bamberger, and Roy J. Epstein. 1995. "Antitrust and Higher Education: Was There a Conspiracy to Restrict Financial Aid?" *Rand Journal of Economics* 26 (Spring): 131–47.

Carroll, Sidney L., and Robert J. Gaston. 1981. "Occupational Restrictions and the Quality of Service Received: Some Evidence." *Southern Economic Journal* 47 (April): 959–76.

Chay, Kenneth Y., and Michael Greenstone. 2001. "Air Quality, Infant Mortality, and the Clean Air Act of 1970." Working paper. University of California, Berkeley, Department of Economics.

———. 2005. "Does Air Quality Matter? Evidence from the Housing Market." *Journal of Political Economy* 113 (April): 376–424.

Chevalier, Judith A., and Dina Mayzlin. 2003. "The Effect of Word of Mouth on Sales: Online Book Reviews." Working Paper 10148. Cambridge, Mass.: National Bureau of Economic Research (December).

Coate, Malcolm B., Richard S. Higgins, and Fred S. McChesney. 1995. "Bureaucracy and Politics in FTC Merger Challenges." In *The Causes and Consequences of Antitrust*, edited by Fred S. McChesney and William F. Shugart II, pp. 213–30. University of Chicago Press.

Cohen, Linda R., and Roger G. Noll. 1991. *The Technology Pork Barrel*. Brookings.

Cohen, Wesley M., and Richard C. Levin. 1989. "Empirical Studies of Innovation and Market Structure." In *Handbook of Industrial Organization*, volume 2, edited by Richard Schmalensee and Robert D. Willig. Amsterdam: Elsevier Publishers.

Congressional Budget Office. 1998. *How Increased Competition from Generic Drugs Has Affected Prices and Returns in the Pharmaceutical Industry.* Washington (July) (www.cbo.gov).

Cowling, Keith, and Dennis C. Mueller. 1978. "The Social Costs of Monopoly Power." *Economic Journal* 88 (December): 727–48.

Crandall, Robert W. 1992. "Corporate Average Fuel Standards." *Journal of Economic Perspectives* 6 (Spring): 171–80.

———. 2005a. "The Remedy for the 'Bottleneck Monopoly' in Telecom: Isolate It, Share It, or Ignore It?" *University of Chicago Law Review* 72 (Winter): 3–25.

———. 2005b. *Competition and Chaos: U.S. Telecommunications Since the 1996 Telecom Act.* Brookings.

Crandall, Robert W., and Harold Furchtgott-Roth. 1996. *Cable TV: Regulation or Competition?* Brookings.

Crandall, Robert W., and John D. Graham. 1989. "The Effect of Fuel Economy Standards on Automobile Safety." *Journal of Law and Economics* 32 (April): 97–118.

Crandall, Robert W., Howard Gruenspecht, Theodore Keeler, and Lester Lave. 1986. *Regulating the Automobile.* Brookings.

Crandall, Robert W., and Jerry A. Hausman. 2000. "Competition in U.S. Telecommunications Services: Effects of the 1996 Legislation." In *Deregulation of Network Industries: What's Next?* edited by Sam Peltzman and Clifford Winston. Washington: American Enterprise Institute and Brookings.

Crandall, Robert W., and Clifford Winston. 2003. "Does Antitrust Policy Improve Consumer Welfare? Assembling the Evidence." *Journal of Economic Perspectives* 17 (Fall): 3-26.

Crawford, Gregory S. 2000. "The Impact of the 1992 Cable Act on Household Demand and Welfare." *Rand Journal of Economics* 31(Autumn): 422–49.

Cropper, Maureen, William N. Evans, S. J. Berardi, M. M. Ducla-Soares, and Paul R. Portney. 1992. "The Determinants of Pesticide Regulation: A Statistical Analysis of EPA Decision Making." *Journal of Political Economy* 100 (February): 175–97.

Dahl, Carol, and Thomas Sterner. 1991. "Analyzing Gasoline Demand Elasticities: A Survey." *Energy Economics* 13 (July): 203–10.

DeLeire, Thomas. 2000. "The Wage and Employment Effects of the Americans with Disabilities Act." *Journal of Human Resources* 35 (Fall): 693–715.

Derthick, Martha, and Paul J. Quirk. 1985. *The Politics of Deregulation.* Brookings.

Douglas, Paul H. 1952. *Economy in the National Government.* University of Chicago Press.

Djankov, Simeon, Rafael LaPorta, Florencio Lopez-de-Silanes, and Andrei Shleifer. 2000. "The Regulation of Entry." Working Paper 7892. Cambridge, Mass.: National Bureau of Economic Research (September).

Early, Dirk W. 1999. "Rent Control, Rental Housing Supply, and the Distribution of Tenant Benefits." *Journal of Urban Economics* 48 (September): 185–204.

Eckbo, B. Espen. 1992. "Mergers and the Value of Antitrust Deterrence." *Journal of Finance* 47 (July): 1005–29.

Ellison, Glenn. 2002. "The Slowdown of the Economics Publishing Process." *Journal of Political Economy* 110 (October): 947–93.

Ellwood, David T. 2001. "The Sputtering Labor Force of the 21st Century: Can Social Policy Help?" In *The Roaring Nineties: Can Full Employment Be Sustained?* edited by Alan Krueger and Robert Solow. New York: Russell Sage Foundation.

Evans, David S., Albert L. Nichols, and Richard Schmalensee. 2005. "U.S. v. Microsoft: Did Consumers Win?" Working Paper 11727. Cambridge, Mass.: National Bureau of Economic Reseach (October).

Evans, Diana. 1994. "Policy and Pork: The Use of Pork Barrel Projects to Build Policy Coalitions in the House of Representatives." *American Journal of Political Science* 38 (November): 894–917.

Faith, Roger L., Donald R. Leavens, and Robert D. Tollison. 1982. "Antitrust Pork Barrel." *Journal of Law and Economics* 25 (October): 329–42.

Feenstra, Robert C. 1992. "How Costly is Protectionism?" *Journal of Economic Perspectives* 6 (Summer): 159–78.

Feldstein, Martin. 2005. "Rethinking Social Insurance." *American Economic Review* 95 (March): 1–24.

Ferguson, Paul R. 1988. *Industrial Economics: Issues and Perspectives.* London: Macmillan.

Frankel, Jeffrey A., and Andrew K. Rose. 2005. "Is Trade Good or Bad for the Environment? Sorting out the Causality." *Review of Economics and Statistics* 87 (February): 85–91.

Friedland, Claire. 2002. "Stigler and Economic Policy." *American Journal of Economics and Sociology* 61: 644–49.

Friedman, Lee S. 1999. "Presidential Address: Peanuts Envy." *Journal of Policy Analysis and Management* 18 (Spring): 211–25.

Friedman, Milton. 1962. *Capitalism and Freedom.* University of Chicago Press.

Garces, Eliana, Duncan Thomas, and Janet Currie. 2002. "Longer-Term Effects of Head Start." *American Economic Review* 92 (September): 999–1012.

Gardner, B. Delworth. 1997. "The Political Economy of Public Land Use." *Journal of Agricultural and Resource Economics* 22: 12–29.

Gardner, Bruce L. 1987. "Causes of U.S. Farm Commodity Programs." *Journal of Political Economy* 95 (April): 290–310.

———. 1992. "Changing Economic Perspectives on the Farm Problem." *Journal of Economic Literature* 30 (March): 62–101.

———. 2002. "Economists and the 2002 Farm Bill: What Is the Value-Added of Policy Analysis?" *Agricultural and Resource Economics Review* 31: 139–46.

Gayer, Ted. 2004. "The Fatality Risks of Sport-Utility Vehicles, Vans, and Pickups Relative to Cars." *Journal of Risk and Uncertainty* 28 (January): 103–33.

Gayer, Ted, James T. Hamilton, and W. Kip Viscusi. 2000. "Private Values of Risk Tradeoffs at Superfund Sites: Housing Market Evidence on Learning about Risk." *Review of Economics and Statistics* 82 (August): 439–51.

Geddes, R. Richard. 2003. *Saving the Mail: How to Solve the Problems of the U.S. Postal Service.* Washington: American Enterprise Institute.

———. 2005. "Reform of the U.S. Postal Service." *Journal of Economic Perspectives* 19 (Summer): 217–32.

Glaeser, Edward L., and Joseph Gyourko. 2003. "The Impact of Zoning on Housing Affordability." *Economic Policy Review* 9 (June): 21–39.

Glaeser, Edward L., and Erzo F. P. Luttmer. 2003. "The Misallocation of Housing under Rent Control." *American Economic Review* 93 (September): 1027–46.

Godek, Paul E. 1985. "Industry Structure and Redistribution through Trade Restrictions." *Journal of Law and Economics* 28 (October): 687–703.

———. 1997. "The Regulation of Fuel Economy and the Demand for 'Light Trucks.'" *Journal of Law and Economics* 40 (October): 495–509.

Gomez-Ibanez, Jose A., and John R. Meyer. 1993. *Going Private: The International Experience with Transport Privatization.* Brookings.

Grabowski, Henry G. 1980. "Regulation and the International Diffusion of Pharmaceuticals." In *The International Supply of Medicines,* edited by Robert B. Helms. Washington: American Enterprise Institute.

Grabowski, Henry G., and John M. Vernon. 1978. "Consumer Product Safety Regulation." *American Economic Review* 68 (May): 284–89.

Gray, Wayne B., and John T. Scholz. 1993. "Does Regulatory Enforcement Work? A Panel Analysis of OSHA Enforcement." *Law and Society Review* 27: 177–214.

Gray, Wayne B., and Ronald J. Shadbegian. 2004. "Optimal Pollution Abatement: Whose Benefits Matter, and How Much?" *Journal of Environmental Economics and Management* 47: 510–34.

Greene, David L. 1998. "Why CAFE Worked." *Energy Policy* 26: 595–613.

Greenstone, Michael. 2002. "The Impacts of Environmental Regulations on Industrial Activity: Evidence from the 1970 and 1977 Clean Air Act Amendments and the Census of Manufactures." *Journal of Political Economy* 110 (December): 1175–219.

Greenstone, Michael, and Justin Gallagher. 2005. "Does Hazardous Waste Matter? Evidence from the Housing Market and the Superfund Program." Working paper. Cambridge, Mass.: MIT Department of Economics (September).

Greenstone, Michael, Paul Oyer, and Annette Vissing-Jorgensen. 2006. "Mandated Disclosure, Stock Returns, and the 1964 Securities Acts Amendments." *Quarterly Journal of Economics* 121 (May): 399–460.

Griffin, James M., and Steven L. Puller, eds. 2005. *Electricity Deregulation: Choices and Challenges.* University of Chicago Press.

Grossman, Gene, and Elhanan Helpman. 2005. "A Protectionist Bias in Majoritarian Politics." *Quarterly Journal of Economics* 120 (November): 1239–82.

Grossman, Michael, Jody L. Sindelar, John Mullahy, and Richard Anderson. 1993. "Alcohol and Cigarette Taxes." *Journal of Economic Perspectives* 7 (Fall): 211–22.

Gruber, Jonathan, and Botond Koszegi. 2002. "A Theory of Government Regulation of Addictive Bads: Optimal Tax Levels and Tax Incidence for Cigarette Excise Taxation." Working Paper 8777. Cambridge, Mass.: National Bureau of Economic Research (February).

Haas-Wilson, Deborah. 1986. "The Effect of Commercial Practice Restrictions: The Case of Optometry." *Journal of Law and Economics* 29 (April): 165–86.

Hahn, Robert W. 1996. "Regulatory Reform: What Do the Government's Numbers Tell Us?" In *Risks, Costs, and Lives Saved: Getting Better Results from Regulation*, edited by Robert W. Hahn. Oxford University Press and AEI Press.

Hahn, Robert W., and Gordon Hester. 1989. "Marketable Permits: Lessons for Theory and Practice." *Ecology Law Quarterly* 16: 380–91.

Hall, Bronwyn H. 1996. "The Private and Social Returns to Research and Development." In *Technology, R&D, and the Economy*, edited by Bruce L. Smith and Claude E. Barfield. Brookings and American Enterprise Institute.

———. 2003. "Business Method Patents, Innovation, and Policy." Working Paper 9717. Cambridge, Mass.: National Bureau of Economic Research.

Hamilton, James T. 2005. *Regulation Through Revelation: The Origin, Politics, and Impacts of the Toxics Release Inventory Program.* Cambridge University Press.

Hamilton, James T., and W. Kip Viscusi. 1999. *Calculating Risks? The Spatial and Political Dimensions of Hazardous Waste Policy.* MIT Press.

Harberger, Arnold C. 1954. "Monopoly and Resource Allocation." *American Economic Review* 44 (May): 77–87.

———. 1971. "Three Postulates for Applied Welfare Economics: An Interpretive Essay." *Journal of Economic Literature* 9 (September): 785–97.

Harris, Richard G. 1994. "Trade and Industrial Policy for a 'Declining' Industry: The Case of the U.S. Steel Industry." In *Empirical Studies of Strategic Trade Policy*, edited by Paul Krugman and Alasdair Smith, pp. 131–56. Published for NBER by the University of Chicago Press.

Hausman, Jerry A. 1981. "Exact Consumer's Surplus and Deadweight Loss." *American Economic Review* 71 (September): 662–76.

———. 1998. "Taxation By Telecommunications Regulation." In *Tax Policy and the Economy*, edited by James M. Poterba. Published for NBER by MIT Press.

Hazilla, Michael, and Raymond J. Kopp. 1990. "Social Cost of Environmental Quality Regulations: A General Equilibrium Analysis." *Journal of Political Economy* 98 (August): 853–73.

Heien, Dale M. 1995. "The Economic Case Against Higher Alcohol Taxes." *Journal of Economic Perspectives* 9 (Winter): 207–09.

Helmberger, Peter, and Yu-Hui Chen. 1994. "Economic Effects of U.S. Dairy Programs." *Journal of Agricultural and Resource Economics* 19 (December): 225–38.

Henderson, J. Vernon. 1996. "Effects of Air Quality Regulation." *American Economic Review* 86 (September): 789–813.

Hirsch, Barry T., Michael L. Wachter, and James W. Gillula. 1999. "Postal Service Compensation and the Comparability Standard." *Research in Labor Economics* 18: 243–79.

Hoffer, George E., Stephen W. Pruitt, and Robert J. Reilly. 1992. "Market Response to Publicly Provided Information: The Case of Automobile Safety." *Applied Economics* 24 (July): 661–67.

Iizuka, Toshiaki, and Ginger Zhe Jin. 2005. "Drug Advertising and Health Habits." Working Paper 11770, Cambridge, Mass.: National Bureau of Economic Research.

Ippolito, Pauline M., and Alan D. Mathios. 1990. "Information, Advertising and Health Choices: A Study of the Cereal Market." *Rand Journal of Economics* 21 (Autumn): 459–80.

———. 1995. "Information and Advertising: The Case of Fat Consumption in the United States." *American Economic Review* 85 (May): 91–95.

Jaffe, Adam B. 1989. "Real Effects of Academic Research." *American Economic Review* 79 (December): 957–70.

———. 2000. "The U.S. Patent System in Transition: Policy Innovation and the Innovation Process." *Research Policy* 29 (April): 531–57.

———. 2002. "Building Programme Evaluation into the Design of Public Research-Support Programmes." *Oxford Review of Economic Policy* 18: 22–34.

Jaffe, Adam B., and Joshua Lerner. 2004. *Innovation and Its Discontents.* Princeton University Press.

Jarrell, Gregg A. 1981. "The Economic Effects of Federal Regulation of the Market for New Security Issues." *Journal of Law and Economics* 24 (December): 613–75.

Jarrell, Gregg A., and Michael Bradley. 1980. "The Economic Effects of Federal and State Regulations of Cash Tender Offers." *Journal of Law and Economics* 23 (October): 371–407.

Jin, Ginger, Andrew Kato, and John List. 2005. "That's News to Me! Information Revelation in Professional Certification Markets." Working paper. University of Maryland, Department of Economics (January).

Johnson, Ronald N., and Gary D. Libecap. 2000. "Political Processes and the Common Pool Problem: The Federal Highway Trust Fund." Working paper. University of Arizona, Department of Economics (June).

Joskow, Paul L. 2001. "California's Electricity Crisis." Working Paper 8442. Cambridge: Mass.: National Bureau of Economic Research (August).

Kalt, Joseph P. 1988. "The Political Economy of Protectionism: Tariffs and Retaliation in the Timber Industry." In *Trade Policy Issues and Empirical Analysis*, edited by Robert Baldwin. University of Chicago Press.

Kaplow, Louis, and Steven Shavell. 2001. "Any Non-welfarist Method of Policy Assessment Violates the Pareto Principle." *Journal of Political Economy* 109 (April): 281–86.

Kellogg, Michael K., John Thorne, and Peter W. Huber. 1992. *Federal Telecommunications Law.* Boston: Little, Brown.

Kessler, Daniel P., and Lawrence F. Katz. 2001. "Prevailing Wage Laws and Construction Labor Markets." *Industrial and Labor Relations Review* 54 (January): 259–74.

Khan, B. Zorina, and Kenneth L. Sokoloff. 2001. "The Early Development of Intellectual Property Institutions in the United States." *Journal of Economic Perspectives* 15 (Summer): 233–46.

Kim, Jinyoung, Sangjoon John Lee, and Gerald Marschke. 2005. "The Influence of University Research on Industrial Innovation." Working paper. State University of New York, Buffalo, Department of Economics (May).

Kleiner, Morris M., and Robert T. Kudrle. 2000. "Does Regulation Affect Economic Outcomes? The Case of Dentistry." *Journal of Law and Economics* 43 (October): 547–82.

Kleit, Andrew N. 2004. "Impacts of Long-Range Increases in Fuel Economy (CAFE) Standards." *Economic Inquiry* 42 (April): 279–94.

Klette, Tor Jakob, Jarle Moen, and Zvi Griliches. 2000. "Do Subsidies to Commercial R&D Reduce Market Failures? Microeconometric Evaluation Studies." *Research Policy* 29 (April): 471–95.

Kniesner, Thomas J., and John D. Leeth. 1999. *Simulating Workplace Safety Policy.* Boston: Kluwer Academic Publishers.

———. 2004. "Data Mining Mining Data: MSHA Enforcement Efforts, Underground Coal Mine Safety, and New Public Health Policy Implications." *Journal of Risk and Uncertainty* 29 (September): 83–111.

Knight, Brian. 2004. "Parochial Interests and the Centralized Provision of Local Public Goods: Evidence from Congressional Voting on Transportation Projects." *Journal of Public Economics* 88: 845–66.

———. 2005. "Estimating the Value of Proposal Power." *American Economic Review* 95 (December): 1639–52.

Kobayashi, Bruce. 2002. "Antitrust, Agency and Amnesty: An Economic Analysis of the Criminal Enforcement of the Antitrust Laws Against Corporations." Law and Economics working paper series 0204. George Mason University School of Law.

Kouliavtsev, Mikhail S. 2004. "Activist Antitrust?" *Journal of Economic Perspectives* 18 (Summer): 223–24.

Kwoka, John E. 1984. "Advertising and the Price and Quality of Optometric Services." *American Economic Review* 74 (March): 211–16.

Lave, Charles, and Lester Lave. 1999. "Fuel Economy and Auto Safety Regulation: Is the Cure Worse than the Disease?" In *Essays in Transportation Economics and Policy: A Handbook in Honor of John R. Meyer,* edited by J. Gomez-Ibanez, W. Tye, and C. Winston, pp. 257–89. Brookings.

Lave, Lester. 1984. "Controlling Contradictions Among Regulations." *American Economic Review* 74 (June): 471–75.

Lazarou, Jason, Bruce H. Pomeranz, and Paul N. Corey. 1998. "Incidence of Adverse Drug Reactions in Hospitalized Patients: A Meta-Analysis of Prospective Studies." *Journal of the American Medical Association* 279 (April 15): 1200–05.

Leal, Donald R. 2006. "Saving Fisheries with Free Markets." *The Milken Institute Review* First Quarter: 56–66.

Levin, Richard, Alvin Klevorick, Richard Nelson, and Sidney Winter. 1987. "Appropriating the Returns from Industrial Research and Development." *Brookings Papers on Economic Activity: Microeconomics* no. 1: 783–820.

Lichtenberg, Frank R. 1988. "The Private R&D Investment Response to Federal Design and Technical Competitions." *American Economic Review* 78 (June): 550–59.

Lipfert, F. W., and S. C. Morris. 2002. "Temporal and Spatial Relations between Age Specific Mortality and Ambient Air Quality in the United States: Regression Results for Counties, 1960–97." *Occupational and Environmental Medicine* 59, no. 3: 156–74.

List, John A., Daniel L. Millimet, and Warren McHone. 2004. "The Unintended Disincentive in the Clean Air Act." *Advances in Economic Analysis and Policy* 4: article 2.

Magat, Wesley, Alan Krupnick, and Winston Harrington. 1986. *Rules in the Making: A Statistical Analysis of Regulatory Agency Behavior.* Washington: Resources for the Future.

Magat, Wesley, and W. Kip Viscusi, eds. 1992. *Informational Approaches to Regulation.* MIT Press.

Mamuneas, Theofanis P., and M. Ishaq Nadiri. 1996. "Public R&D Policies and Cost Behavior of the U.S. Manufacturing Industries." *Journal of Public Economics* 63 (December): 57–81.

Mannering, Fred, and Clifford Winston. 1995. "Automobile Air Bags in the 1990s: Market Failure or Market Efficiency?" *Journal of Law and Economics* 38 (October): 265–79.

Mansfield, Edwin. 1986. "Patents and Innovation: An Empirical Study." *Management Science* 32: 173–81.

———. 1991. "Academic Research and Industrial Innovation." *Research Policy* 20: 1–12.

Mathios, Alan D. 2000. "The Impact of Mandatory Disclosure Laws on Product Choices: An Analysis of the Salad Dressing Market." *Journal of Law and Economics* 43 (October): 651–77.

Mathios, Alan, and Mark Plummer. 1989. "The Regulation of Advertising by the Federal Trade Commission." *Research in Law and Economics* 12 (Autumn): 77–93.

Mayer, Christopher, and Todd Sinai. 2003. "Network Effects, Congestion Externalities, and Air Traffic Delays: Or Why Not All Delays Are Evil." *American Economic Review* 93 (September): 1194–1215.

Mazzoleni, Roberto, and Richard R. Nelson. 1998. "The Benefits and Costs of Strong Patent Protection: A Contribution to the Current Debate." *Research Policy* 27 (July): 273–84.

McCubbins, Mathew D., Roger G. Noll, and Barry R. Weingast. 1987. "Administrative Procedures as Instruments of Political Control." *Journal of Law, Economics, and Organization* 3 (Fall): 243–77.

McFadden, Daniel. 2001. "California Needs Deregulation Done Right," *Wall Street Journal*, February 13, 2001.

Meyer, Bruce D., W. Kip Viscusi, and David L. Durbin. 1995. "Workers' Compensation and Injury Duration: Evidence from a Natural Experiment." *American Economic Review* 85 (June): 322–39.

Moffitt, Robert, ed. 2003. *Means-Tested Transfer Programs in the United States.* University of Chicago Press.

Moore, Michael J., and W. Kip Viscusi. 1990. *Compensation Mechanisms for Job Risks: Wages, Workers' Compensation, and Product Liability.* Princeton University Press.

Morrison, Steven A. 1987. "The Equity and Efficiency of Runway Pricing." *Journal of Public Economics* 34 (October): 45–60.

———. 1990. "The Value of Amtrak." *Journal of Law and Economics* 33 (October): 361–82.

———. 1996. "Airline Mergers: A Longer View." *Journal of Transport Economics and Policy* 30 (September): 237–50.

Morrison, Steven A., and Clifford Winston. 1989. "Enhancing the Performance of the Deregulated Air Transportation System." *Brookings Papers on Economic Activity: Microeconomics*: 61–112.

———. 1995. *The Evolution of the Airline Industry.* Brookings.

———. 1996. "Causes and Consequences of Airline Fare Wars." *Brookings Papers on Economic Activity: Microeconomics:* 85–123.

———. 2005. "Another Look at Appropriate Policy toward Air Travel Delays." Working paper. Brookings (August).

Morrison, Steven A., Clifford Winston, and Tara Watson. 1999. "Fundamental Flaws of Social Regulation: The Case of Airplane Noise." *Journal of Law and Economics* 42 (October): 723–43.

Mukamal, Kenneth J., and others. 2003. "Roles of Drinking Pattern and Type of Alcohol Consumed in Coronary Heath Disease in Men." *New England Journal of Medicine* 348 (January 9): 109–18.

Nelson, Robert H. 2000. *A Burning Issue: A Case for Abolishing the U.S. Forest Service.* Lanham, Md.: Rowman & Littlefield Publishers.

Neumark, David, and Wendy Stock. 2001 "The Effects of Race and Sex Discrimination Laws." Working Paper 8215. Cambridge, Mass.: National Bureau of Economic Research (April).

Newell, Richard G., Adam B. Jaffe, and Robert N. Stavins. 1999. "The Induced Innovation Hypothesis and Energy-Saving Technological Change." *Quarterly Journal of Economics* 114 (August): 941–75.

Newmark, Craig M. 1988. "Does Horizontal Price Fixing Raise Price? A Look at the Bakers of Washington Case." *Journal of Law and Economics* 31 (October): 469–84.

Noll, Roger G. 1989a. "Economic Perspectives on the Politics of Regulation." In *Handbook of Industrial Organization*, vol. 2, edited by Richard Schmalensee and Robert Willig. Amsterdam: North-Holland Press.

Noll, Roger G. 1989b. "The Economic Theory of Regulation after a Decade of Deregulation: Comments." *Brookings Papers on Economic Activity: Microeconomics:* 48–58.

Oi, Walter Y. 1974. "On the Economics of Industrial Safety." *Law and Contemporary Problems* 38 (Summer-Autumn): 669–99.

Okun, Arthur M. 1975. *Equality and Efficiency: The Big Tradeoff.* Brookings.

Olson, Mancur. 1965. *The Logic of Collective Action.* Harvard University Press.

Olson, Mary K. 2002. "How Have User Fees Affected the FDA?" *Regulation* 25 (Spring): 20–25.

O'Toole, Randal. 2002. "Money to Burn?" *Regulation* 25 (Winter): 16–20.

Pashigian, B. Peter. 1985. "Environmental Regulation: Whose Self-Interests are Being Protected?" *Economic Inquiry* 23 (October): 551–84.

———. 2000. "Teaching Microeconomics in Wonderland." Working paper 161. George J. Stigler Center for the Study of the Economy and the State, University of Chicago (July).

Peltzman, Sam. 1973. "An Evaluation of Consumer Protection Legislation: The 1962 Drug Amendments." *Journal of Political Economy* 81 (September): 1049–91.

———. 1975. "The Effects of Automobile Safety Regulation." *Journal of Political Economy* 83 (August): 677–725.

———. 1981. "The Effects of FTC Advertising Regulation." *Journal of Law and Economics* 24 (December): 403–48.

———. 1987. "The Health Effects of Mandatory Prescriptions." *Journal of Law and Economics* 30 (October): 207–38.

———. 1989. "The Economic Theory of Regulation after a Decade of Deregulation." *Brookings Papers on Economic Activity: Microeconomics:* 1–59.

———. 2005. "Aaron Director's Influence on Antitrust Policy." *Journal of Law and Economics* 48 (October): 313–30.

Philipson, Tomas J., Ernst Berndt, Adrian Gottschalk, and Matthew Strobeck. 2005. "Assessing the Safety and Efficacy of the FDA: The Case of the Prescription Drug User Fee Acts." Working paper 199. George J. Stigler Center for the Study of the Economy and the State, University of Chicago.

Poitras, Marc, and Daniel Sutter. 2002. "Policy Ineffectiveness or Offsetting Behavior? An Analysis of Vehicle Safety Inspections." *Southern Economic Journal* 68 (July): 922–34.

Portney, Paul, ed. 1990. *Public Policies for Environmental Protection.* Washington: Resources for the Future.

Portney, Paul, Ian W. H. Parry, Howard K. Gruenspecht, and Winston Harrington. 2003. "The Economics of Fuel Economy Standards." *Journal of Economic Perspectives* 17 (Fall): 203–17.

Posner, Eric A. 2001. "Controlling Agencies with Cost-Benefit Analysis: A Positive Political Theory Perspective." John M. Olin Law & Economics Working Paper 119. University of Chicago.

Posner, Richard A. 1993. "Nobel Laureate: Ronald Coase and Methodology." *Journal of Economic Perspectives* 7 (Fall): 195–210.

Poterba, James M. 1993. "Global Warming Policy: A Public Finance Perspective." *Journal of Economic Perspectives* 7 (Fall): 47–63.

Quigley, John M., and Steven Raphael. 2005. "Regulation and the High Cost of Housing in California." *American Economic Review* 95 (May): 323–28.

Rausser, Gordon. 1992. "Predatory Versus Productive Government: The Case of U.S. Agricultural Policies." *Journal of Economic Perspectives* 6 (Summer): 133–57.

Reynolds, Clark W., and Robert K. McCleery. 1988. "The Political Economy of Immigration Law: Impact of Simpson-Rodino on the Unites States and Mexico." *Journal of Economic Perspectives* 2 (Summer): 117–31.

Ringold, Debra Jones, and John E. Calfee. 1990. "What Can We Learn from the Informational Content of Cigarette Advertising? A Reply and Further Analysis." *Journal of Public Policy and Marketing* 9: 30–41.

Robinson, Sherman, Maureen Kilkenny, and Irma Adelman. 1989. "The Effect of Agricultural Trade Liberalization on the U.S. Economy: Projections to 1991." In *Macroeconomic Consequences of Farm Support Policies*, edited by Andrew B. Stoeckel, David Vincent, and Sandy Cuthbertson. Duke University Press.

Romano, Roberta. 2005. "The Sarbanes-Oxley Act and the Making of Quack Corporate Governance." *Yale Law Journal* 114 (May): 1521–1611.

Sauer, Raymond D., and Keith B. Leffler. 1990. "Did the Federal Trade Commission's Advertising Substantiation Program Promote More Credible Advertising?" *American Economic Review* 80 (March): 191–203.

Schmalensee, Richard, and others. 1998. "An Interim Evaluation of Sulfur Dioxide Emissions Trading." *Journal of Economic Perspectives* 12 (Summer): 53–68.

Schroeter, John R., Scott L. Smith, and Steven R. Cox. 1987. "Advertising and Competition in Routine Legal Service Markets: An Empirical Investigation." *Journal of Industrial Economics* 36 (September): 49–60.

Schultze, Charles L. 1977. *The Public Use of Private Interest.* Brookings.

Schuman, Lawrence, James D. Reitzes, and Robert P. Rogers. 1997. "In the Matter of Weyerhauser Company: The Use of a Hold-Separate Order in a Merger with Horizontal and Vertical Effects." *Journal of Regulatory Economics* 11: 271–89.

Sider, Hal. 1983. "Safety and Productivity in Underground Coal Mining." *Review of Economics and Statistics* 65 (May): 225–33.

Simon, Carol J. 1989. "The Effect of the 1933 Securities Act on Investor Infor-
    mation and the Performance of New Issues." *American Economic Review* 79
    (June): 295–318.
Small, Kenneth A., Clifford Winston, and Carol A. Evans. 1989. *Road Work: A
    New Highway Pricing and Investment Policy.* Brookings.
Small, Kenneth A., Clifford Winston, and Jia Yan. 2006. "Differentiated Road
    Pricing, Express Lanes, and Carpools: Exploiting Heterogeneous Preferences in
    Policy Design." *Brookings Wharton Papers on Urban Affairs.*
Smith, Robert S. 1992. "Have OSHA and Workers' Compensation Made the
    Workplace Safer?" In *Research Frontiers in Industrial Relations and Human
    Resources*, edited by David Lewin, Olivia S. Mitchell, and Peter D. Sherer.
    Ithaca, N.Y.: Industrial Relations Research Association.
Smithson, Charles W., and Christopher R. Thomas. 1988. "Measuring the Cost
    to Consumers of Product Defects: The Value of Lemon Insurance." *Journal of
    Law and Economics* 31 (October): 485–502.
Sobel, Russel S. 1999. "Theory and Evidence on the Political Economy of the
    Minimum Wage." *Journal of Political Economy* 107 (August): 761–85.
Sproul, Michael F. 1993. "Antitrust and Prices." *Journal of Political Economy* 101
    (August): 741–54.
Squires, Dale, and James Kirkley. 1991. "Production Quota in Multiproduct
    Pacific Fisheries." *Journal of Environmental Economics and Management* 21
    (September): 109–26.
Stigler, George J. 1966. "The Economic Effects of the Antitrust Laws." *Journal of
    Law and Economics* 9 (October): 225–58.
———. 1982. "The Economists and the Problem of Monopoly." *American Eco-
    nomic Review* 72 (May): 1–11.
Stiglitz, Joseph E. 1998. "The Private Uses of Public Interests: Incentives and Insti-
    tutions." *Journal of Economic Perspectives* 12 (Spring): 3–22.
Sunstein, Cass. 2001. "Regulating Risks after ATA." John M. Olin Law & Eco-
    nomics Working Paper 127. University of Chicago.
Sutherland, Ronald J. 1991. "Market Barriers to Energy-Efficient Investments."
    Energy Journal 12: 15–34.
Teisl, Mario F., Brian Roe, and Robert L. Hicks. 2002. "Can Eco-Labels Tune a
    Market? Evidence from Dolphin-Safe Labeling." *Journal of Environmental Eco-
    nomics and Management* 43 (May): 339–59.
Thomas, Lacy Glenn. 1988. "Revealed Bureaucratic Preference: Priorities of the
    Consumer Product Safety Commission." *Rand Journal of Economics* 19
    (Spring): 102–13.
Trejo, Stephen J. 1991. "The Effects of Overtime Pay Regulation on Worker
    Compensation." *American Economic Review* 81 (September): 719–40.
U.S. Government Accountability Office. 2005. *Economic Performance.* GAO-05-
    796SP (July).

Varian, Hal. 1993. "What Use is Economic Theory?" University of Michigan, Department of Economics (May 4).

Viscusi, W. Kip. 1985. "Consumer Behavior and the Safety Effects of Product Safety Regulation." *Journal of Law and Economics* 28 (October): 527–53.

———. 1986. "The Impact of Occupational Safety and Health Regulation, 1973–1983." *Rand Journal of Economics* 17 (Winter): 567–80.

———. 1993. "The Value of Risks to Life and Health." *Journal of Economic Literature* 31 (December): 1912–46.

———. 2002. *Smoke-Filled Rooms: A Postmortem on the Tobacco Deal.* University of Chicago Press.

Viscusi, W. Kip, and Joseph E. Aldy. 2003. "The Value of Statistical Life: A Critical Review of Market Estimates throughout the World." *Journal of Risk and Uncertainty* 27 (August): 5–76.

Viscusi, W. Kip, Joseph E. Harrington, and John M. Vernon. 2005. *Economics of Regulation and Antitrust,* 4th ed. MIT Press.

Viscusi, W. Kip, and Wesley Magat. 1987. *Learning About Risk: Consumer and Worker Responses to Hazard Information.* Harvard University Press.

Vogelsang, Ingo. 2002. "Incentive Regulation and Competition in Public Utility Markets: A 20-Year Perspective." *Journal of Regulatory Economics* 22 (July): 5–27.

Wallsten, Scott J. 2000. "The Effects of Government-Industry R&D Programs on Private R&D: The Case of the Small Business Innovation Research Program." *Rand Journal of Economics* 31 (Spring): 82–100.

Wattles, George M. 1973. "The Rates and Costs of the United States Postal Service." *Journal of Law and Economics* 16 (April): 89–117.

Weil, David. 1996. "If OSHA Is So Bad, Why Is Compliance So Good?" *Rand Journal of Economics* 27 (Autumn): 618–40.

Weingast, Barry R., and Mark J. Moran. 1983. "Bureaucratic Discretion or Congressional Control? Regulatory Policymaking by the Federal Trade Commission." *Journal of Political Economy* 91 (October): 765–800.

Werden, Gregory J. 2004. "Activist Antitrust?" *Journal of Economic Perspectives* 18 (Summer): 224–25.

White, Lawrence. 2002. "Credit and Credibility," *New York Times*, February 24, 2002.

White, Michelle J. 2004. "The 'Arms Race' on American Roads: The Effect of Sport Utility Vehicles and Pickup Trucks on Traffic Safety." *Journal of Law and Economics* 47 (October): 333–55.

Wiggins, Steven N. 1981. "Product Quality Regulation and New Drug Introductions: Some New Evidence from the 1970s." *Review of Economics and Statistics* 63 (November): 615–19.

Willig, Robert D. 1976. "Consumer's Surplus Without Apology." *American Economic Review* 66 (September): 589–97.

Winston, Clifford. 1993. "Economic Deregulation: Days of Reckoning for Micro-economists." *Journal of Economic Literature* 31 (September): 1263–89.

———. 1998. "U.S. Industry Adjustment to Economic Deregulation." *Journal of Economic Perspectives* 12 (Summer): 89–110.

———. 2000. "Government Failure in Urban Transportation." *Fiscal Studies* 21 (December): 403-25.

Winston, Clifford, and Ashley Langer. 2006. "The Effect of Government Spending on Road Users' Congestion Costs." *Journal of Urban Economics*, forthcoming.

Winston, Clifford, and Vikram Maheshri. 2006a. "On the Social Desirability of Urban Rail Transit Systems." *Journal of Urban Economics*, forthcoming.

———. 2006b. "Persistent Inefficiencies of Public Policy." Working paper. Brookings.

Winston, Clifford, Vikram Maheshri, and Fred Mannering. 2006. "A Test of the Offset Hypothesis Using Disaggregate Data: The Case of Airbags and Antilock Brakes." *Journal of Risk and Uncertainty* 32 (March): 83–99.

Winston, Clifford, and Chad Shirley. 1998. *Alternate Route: Toward Efficient Urban Transportation.* Brookings.

Wolf, Charles, Jr. 1979. "A Theory of Nonmarket Failure: Framework for Imple-mentation Analysis." *Journal of Law and Economics* 22 (April): 107–39.

Zettelmeyer, Florian, Fiona Scott Morton, and Jorge Silva-Risso. 2001. "Cowboys or Cowards: Why Are Internet Car Prices Lower?" Working Paper 8667. Cam-bridge, Mass.: National Bureau of Economic Research (December).

———. 2005. "How the Internet Lowers Prices: Evidence from the Matched Sur-vey and Auto Transactions Data." Working Paper 11515. Cambridge, Mass.: National Bureau of Economic Research (July).

Index

AARP (American Association of Retired Persons), 89

Advertising: benefits, 77, 96; product labeling, 33–34; regulation, 27–28, 29–31, 39–40, 96

Agricultural Adjustment Act, 23

Agriculture, economic regulation of: efforts to improve government policy approach, 94–95, 99; government intervention rationale, 23; subsidy programs, 22–24, 79, 82, 94–95; trade regulation, 24

Airline industry: aircraft noise pollution, 46, 78; airport congestion, 67; compensation for bumped travelers, 77; Computer Reservations System, 32; federal management, 62, 66–67; passenger delays, 62

Air pollution, 44–46; allowance trading, 50, 51; command-and-control regulation, 42; cost-benefit analysis of regulation, 45–46; government failure in policies to control, 75; government intervention rationale, 42; market forces in controlling externality costs, 78;

market-oriented approaches to control, 100

Allowance trading, 50, 51

Amtrak, 70–71

Antitrust law: consumer welfare outcomes, 14; cost-benefit analysis of policy outcomes, 20–21; deterrence effects of prosecutions, 19–20, 73; efforts to improve government policy approach, 94; enforcement authority, 14; enforcement costs, 20–21; government failure, 73, 79–80; international comparison, 19; merger challenges, 18–19, 21; outcomes of federal antimonopoly lawsuits, 16–17; outcomes of federal prosecution of collusion, 17–18, 21, 73; rationale, 3, 14; recommendations for improving government policies, 98; research needs, 98; *vs.* market-based controls, 20

Army Corps of Engineers, 67–68

AT&T monopolization case, 16–17

Auction of public goods, $100n$

Automobiles: emissions regulation, 44–46; energy efficiency, 47–49, 80; hybrid

J O I N T C E N T E R

AEI-BROOKINGS JOINT CENTER FOR REGULATORY STUDIES